T0204971

LAW OF
ATTRACTION

LAW OF ATTRACTION

MANIFEST YOUR PERFECT LIFE

EMILY ANDERSON

SIRIUS

SIRIUS

This edition published in 2024 by Sirius Publishing, a division of
Arcturus Publishing Limited,
26/27 Bickels Yard, 151–153 Bermondsey Street,
London SE1 3HA

Copyright © Arcturus Holdings Limited

All rights reserved. No part of this publication may be reproduced,
stored in a retrieval system, or transmitted, in any form or by any
means, electronic, mechanical, photocopying, recording or
otherwise, without written permission in accordance with the
provisions of the Copyright Act 1956 (as amended). Any person or
persons who do any unauthorised act in relation to this publication
may be liable to criminal prosecution and civil claims for damages.

ISBN: 978-1-3988-4357-8
AD011465UK

Printed in China

Contents

INTRODUCTION

The law of attraction is one of many spiritual laws of the universe that explain how life works. Also called the law of mirroring, it means that *like attracts like*, and everything in your life is a reflection of your vibrational frequency. According to this law, the frequency you emanate depends on your state of being, which comes about due to the emotions you feel, which are created by your thoughts and beliefs about yourself and others, as well as events in your life.

This fundamental law of nature is based on ancient knowledge that grew popular from the late 1800s onwards via the New Thought Movement, which this book will explore in more detail. Awareness of the law of attraction has expanded in the last few decades to include hundreds of books by best-selling authors such as Louise Hay, Dr Wayne Dyer, Mike Dooley, Gabrielle Bernstein, and Esther and Jerry Hicks, plus countless courses and films, including the Rhonda Byrne documentary *The Secret* (2006) and Dyer's movie *The Shift* (2009).

Many experts in the field of metaphysics state that our *thoughts create our reality*, and that what you think about and focus on, you become or attract. So if you want a successful, fulfilling and happy life full of love, good health and prosperity, you have to think the right thoughts to bring this into being. By cultivating positive thinking, stating your intentions and elevating your emotions, you align your energy with that of the loving, expansive universe (also called God, Source, Infinite Intelligence, Divinity and other names in this book) so you can receive the gifts it has for you. This doesn't just mean material items, such as a beautiful home or an expensive new car, although these can also be manifested. It's about finding fulfilment in your relationships, enjoying the career of your dreams and experiencing an overall richer, deeper, healthier, more creative and exciting life.

History of the law of attraction

It is not a new notion that our thoughts become things. Everything that humans have ever created started out as a thought in someone's mind. Great thinkers and writers in ancient Christian, Hindu and Buddhist scriptures explained that our thoughts are able to shape our world, and that what we give, we receive. The Buddha (563-483 BCE) shared that, 'All that we are is a result of what we have thought.' The Bible is full of the same message, such as in Proverbs 23:7, when it says, 'As a man thinketh in his heart so is he.' Jesus Christ taught that it's our beliefs and our words that manifest our reality, when he said, 'Believe and ye shall receive,' and, 'By your words ye are justified and by your words ye are condemned.'

The great Roman emperor Marcus Aurelius said, 'Our life is what our thoughts make it.' In fact, many of history's greatest artists, scientists and philosophers knew about the law of attraction, including Plato and Socrates, Shakespeare and Beethoven, Newton, Edison and Einstein. Napoleon is quoted as saying, 'Whatever the mind of man can conceive and believe, it can achieve.'

From the early 19th century, a group of theologians, philosophers, teachers and writers, mostly from the New England area of the United States, began exploring and sharing theories and methods to live according to the law of attraction. Earlier influences of the movement include the founder of the 18th-century New Church, Emanuel Swedenborg, who wrote

about the Bible in a new, metaphysical way, exploring the nature of reality, cause and effect, and other philosophical aspects of existence.

Poet, essayist and philosopher Ralph Waldo Emerson is sometimes given the title 'the father of New Thought' for his transcendentalism movement, with its belief that people are inherently good and, when left to be self-reliant, can transcend their material circumstances. The New Thought movement took Emerson's philosophical idealism and added experiential proof of idealistic practice, often through the power of hypnosis, using words to influence outcomes.

New Thought mixed together American Christianity, Hinduism and other Eastern beliefs, along with transcendentalism and mesmerism – the theory of energy transference between animate and inanimate objects popularized by German physician Franz Mesmer. This new metaphysical understanding of the Bible stated that God, or Divine or Infinite Intelligence, is in all things; is a force for good; and that humanity's true essence is this divinity, but negative thinking limits our divine nature. Aiming to transform people's lives for the better, various teachers shared this ancient wisdom through books and lectures about positive thinking, creative visualization and personal empowerment. The movement grew to include many new churches, colleges set up specifically to study this new brand of philosophy, and publishing companies to help spread the word throughout the 19th and 20th centuries.

Another founder of this movement is American inventor Phineas Quimby (1802-1866) after his practical work on psychosomatic illness and the ability to affect your wellbeing with your thoughts. Inspired by a lecture by Charles Poyen, a French mesmerist or 'magnetiser', Quimby discovered that excitement could dull pain. He began a lengthy study into the significant ways that the mind affects the body, including the detrimental impact of negative and false beliefs about oneself. Quimby's work attracted a lot of attention from those wanting help with their own healing, including Mary Baker Eddy, whose long-term back condition was cured by Quimby's mind-transforming healing techniques. Eddy went on to study and share her healing story and techniques, publishing *Science and Health* in 1875, explaining that the power of the mind could cure illness and restore good health. Her work founded the Christian Science church denomination, heavily influenced by New Thought principles. The following year she opened the Massachusetts Metaphysical College, where many leading lights in the movement studied.

Around the same time, the Russian-born psychic, medium and spiritual teacher Madame Helena Blavatsky (1831-1891) was travelling the world sharing her skills and wisdom about life's mysteries. Her most influential book, *The Secret Doctrine*, explained that 'The Universe is worked and guided from within outwards.' She explored the theory that we are who we believe we are, that our self-perceptions influence our reality and identity, and that our thoughts can change our future for the better.

Toward the end of the 19th century and into the 20th, many authors published books popularizing and developing these ideas. American author Prentice Mulford (1834-1891) wrote in depth about his own and others' first-hand experiences of the law of attraction in action – he was possibly the first to use the term. His books, including *Thoughts Are Things*, *The Gift of Understanding* and *Your Forces and How to Use Them*, form the basis of contemporary manifestation principles, where the right kind of thinking can affect not only our health but also life opportunities and material gains. He was vastly ahead of others in describing the oneness of humanity at a spiritual level and extolling the benefits of mindfulness.

In 1901-2, Harvard University psychologist and philosopher William James took his work to Edinburgh University in Scotland, and delivered a series of natural

theology lectures based on his book *The Varieties of Religious Experience: A Study in Human Nature*. James developed his philosophy of pragmatism, where words and thought are considered tools for prediction, problem-solving and action, rather than simply to describe or represent reality.

Uniquely for this era, there were many women developing and leading the New Thought movement. Mary Baker Eddy's student theologist, the feminist and spiritual teacher Emma Curtis Hopkins, branched out after two years to develop her own form of metaphysical idealism, shared in her first book *Class Lessons, 1888*, based on her notes from Eddy's classes. She wrote a vast body of titles on the subject and was a highly acclaimed and charismatic public speaker, with many documented cases of attendees to her lectures being healed almost instantly. Her methods encompassed various mystical traits of Gnosticism, theosophy and early Christian and Eastern teachings, as explained in her last book, *High Mysticism* (1924).

Along with another of Eddy's students, Mary H Plunkett, Hopkins founded the Emma Curtis Hopkins College of Christian Science, in Chicago, with Hopkins as teacher and Plunkett the president and business administrator. Quite rightly, Hopkins became known as 'the mother of New Thought' and the 'teacher of teachers' of many future leaders in the movement. It was Hopkins' students who went on to formally create the national movement and form the International New Thought Association in 1918, of which Hopkins was voted the first president.

Hopkins' notable students, who went on to start their own churches and schools, included Annie Rix Militz, who founded the Home of Truth; Malinda E Cramer and Nona L Brooks who together founded the Church of Divine Science; and Charles and Myrtle Fillmore who started the Unity School of Christianity after their studies at Hopkins College. Many writers were also inspired by Emma Hopkins, including Ella Wheeler Wilcox, a New Thought poet; H Emilie Cady, who wrote the Unity textbook *Lessons in Truth*; and Elizabeth Towne who went on to become Editor of *The Nautilus Magazine of New Thought*. Towne became a publisher of other New Thought titles, such as *Prosperity Through*

Thought Force (1907) by Bruce MacLelland, in which he summarized the principle behind the law of attraction, stating, 'You are what you think, not what you think you are.' This was followed, in 1910, by Wallace D Wattles' *The Science of Getting Rich*, which set out a clear method for attracting wealth according to New Thought principles, including describing the use of creative visualization – imagining all your dreams in detail to bring them into being.

Another popular female author of New Thought ideas in the early 20th century was the American artist, illustrator and Unity church teacher Florence Scovel Shinn, who self-published her first book, *The Game of Life and How to Play It*, in 1925. As with her later titles, *Your Word Is Your Wand* (1928) and *The Secret Door to Success* (1940), Shinn shares a metaphysical understanding of the Bible, where the

laws of success, fulfilment and prosperity come from letting the God consciousness within us lead the way. Her work, quoted extensively in this book, includes many anecdotes of her plentiful clients who used her insights, awareness and affirmations to turn their lives around with great success.

One of the most prolific writers in the New Thought movement, William Walker Atkinson (1862-1932), stumbled across the law of attraction ideas when, as a lawyer, work stress led to his mental and physical collapse. Inspired by the movement, he launched another New Thought magazine, started a school for mental science and wrote over 100 books, including *Thought Vibration: The Law of Attraction in the Thought World*. The book, published in 1906, fully explored the premise that 'like attracts like.' Often drawing on Hindu teachings about willpower, concentration and personal magnetism, his work introduced the concept of raising our vibrational frequency through our thoughts and actions in order to attract positive experiences and success.

Around the same time, American author, philosopher and businessman Charles Haanel (1866-1949) was also developing ideas of attracting abundance and prosperity through the power of positivity in his books *The New Psychology* and *The Master Key System*. He gave practical techniques to

master visualization and cultivate an optimistic and generous mindset to boost your chances of not only financial success, but a happy and fulfilling life all round.

Another best-selling New Thought author was Illinois-born Ralph Waldo Trine (1866-1958), who strongly believed that positive thinking could transform your life if you worked at it with specific techniques and daily habits. His books, including *In Tune with the Infinite* (1897), *Character-Building Thought Power* (1900) and *The Higher Powers of Mind and Spirit* (1917), give readers the knowledge and skills to rise above their everyday struggles to become conscious of their own divinity, 'with all its attendant riches, and glories, and powers'.

Trine's work inspired another writer, journalist Oliver Napoleon Hill, whose hugely successful book *Think and Grow Rich*, published in 1937, has now been made into a film featuring Bob Proctor, one of the experts in the documentary *The Secret*. One of the

best-selling books of all time, selling over 60 million copies, *Think and Grow Rich* analyzed the habits of over 500 self-made millionaires in America, including motor-industry pioneer Henry Ford and billionaire steel magnate Andrew Carnegie. Hill's research showed that often expectation – of struggle, success or unlimited potential – played a large part in what happened in your life. As Hill said, 'If you do not see riches in your imagination, you will never see them in your bank balance.'

Having learned a lot from Hill's work, another American writer, William Clement Stone (1902-2002), went on to emphasize that we can only achieve what we desire as long as we are confident in our ability to do so. His motivational phrase, 'If you think you can, do,' led to him taking full advantage of all opportunities that came his way, making him a popular self-help author and philanthropist. Having come from a family seriously in debt from his father's gambling losses, he brought forth the idea that our

failures, difficulties and even traumas can be used as stepping stones for success. He explained that with the perspective of gratitude for the experience, rather than feeling like a victim, life could be transformed into something much more positive.

Current law of attraction experts

Cultivating an 'attitude of gratitude' remains one of the key ways to attract greater things into your life, shared by many contemporary motivational writers and speakers who came after these pioneers. These include Gabrielle Bernstein, Dr Joe Dispenza and Dr Wayne Dyer, as well as celebrities such as Oprah Winfrey, Denzel Washington and Jim Carrey.

Building on the concepts of the New Thought writers above, Dyer wrote *Your Erroneous Zones*, published in 1976, his first of over 40 books including *Manifest Your Destiny*, *Excuses Begone!*, and *Change Your Thoughts, Change Your Life*, about transforming negative thoughts to turn your life around. Dyer used key New Thought spiritual principles himself, to build his hugely successful writing and speaking career from humble beginnings.

Not long after, in 1984, Louise Hay released her book *You Can Heal Your Life*, which expanded Florence Scovel Shinn's ideas linking ill health to negative self-talk and unexpressed emotions, with a full directory of health issues along with their mental and emotional causes. Like Shinn, Hay gave a path out of victimhood to healing and happiness via positive affirmations, as well as exercises to boost self-love. Hay started her own publishing company off the back of the book's success, publishing countless other manifesting books helping people change their thinking and their lives according to the law of attraction.

But it was the Rhonda Byrne film *The Secret*, released in 2006, that really caught the wider public's attention for learning how to manifest a better life. It shared so many different experts' tips for attracting prosperity, good health and happiness that their wisdom couldn't be ignored. Highly acclaimed writers Mike Dooley and Bob Proctor; Michael B Beckwith, founder of the Agape International Spiritual Center in California; motivational author, speaker and life coach Jack Canfield; and channeller Esther Hicks are all still tireless in their sharing of the law of attraction secrets to a successful, happy and fulfilled life. Hicks and her late husband Jerry wrote many books about the law of attraction, including *Ask and It Is Given*, after they received channelled messages from Source energy, which the pair called Abraham. Now, Esther travels the world sharing this same wisdom from Source under the name Abraham-Hicks.

What all the law of attraction experts agree is that God/Source energy/Christ consciousness is within us all, just as it is in all life, all around us, past, present and future. This means everything is connected, part of the same infinite intelligence. All that exists comes out of this superconscious divine mind, where every good idea has already manifested. Physicists are still exploring this theory, called the quantum field, where everything is energy, constantly moving, changing and affecting everything; the microcosm affecting the macrocosm.

Writer and teacher Lorie Ladd talks about this in her YouTube videos and her book *The Divine Design*. She says, 'The quantum field means that everything is possible in any moment, right now. Think about something you love, you could pull that in. You could attract anger, fear, joy, love. Everything's available in the quantum field within you – because you have the entire universe within you.'

You just have to connect to this divine consciousness to work with it, to feel what it has in store for you and to allow it to lead you towards the creative, joyful and fulfilling life of your dreams. By quieting the rational mind, following your intuitive hunches and thinking the right kind of thoughts, you can become a magnet for all you desire. This book will show you how to align your mind, words, intentions and actions with this infinite wisdom to allow your divinely guided life to unfold.

CHAPTER 1

POSITIVE THOUGHTS

Although invisible, thoughts are an incredibly powerful force. They influence everything from our health and wellbeing to our careers, prosperity and relationships. Thoughts form intentions, goals and plans, create emotions, ignite desires and spur actions. They can create something new or keep us stuck in the past. Thoughts can change the course of your life, for better or for worse.

Over the last couple of centuries, science has proven that the power of thought can change reality. Quantum physicist Max Planck (1858-1947) noticed that, 'When you change the way you look at things, the things you look at change.' Not long after, Albert Einstein (1879-1955) demonstrated that the act of observing an experiment can change the results. The observer's thoughts, expectations and assumptions about how the experiment will play out actually affect the outcome. This means that our minds can affect, even create, our world.

More recently, the work of Bruce Lipton PhD has shown that our minds affect not only our mental and emotional states but our physical health in every way, healing the body of chronic conditions and injuries through the power of belief. His research proves earlier New Thought theories: that we are not just a product of our biology, genetics and DNA; we are, in fact, what we believe.

We make our own luck through the power of our mind. Think thoughts of success and prosperity, dream confidently of doing well without any conflicting beliefs getting in the way, and act in good faith that all you desire will all manifest – and it will. As the proponents of New Thought repeatedly demonstrated and shared in their work, this is the law of attraction in action, where *thoughts become things*.

According to Prentice Mulford, in his book *Your Forces and How to Use Them*, thoughts are a very real and dynamic force: 'Every thought, spoken or unspoken, is a thing, a substance, as real, though invisible, as water or metal ... Every plan or invention clearly seen in thoughts is ... as real a thing as the wood, stone, iron or other substance in which afterward it may be embodied and made visible to the body's eye, and made to work results on the physical stratum of life.'

Furthermore, 'Mind is "magnetic"', says Mulford, 'because it attracts to itself whatever thought it fixes itself upon, or whatever it opens itself to.' Start thinking about anything and you'll find the train of thoughts continues in the same vein until you become fully aware of them. Positive thoughts raise your energy, help plans go well and enable you to have a happy life. Thoughts of a more negative nature can bring you down, make you mentally and physically unwell, and create situations that might have been avoided had your perspective been different. To attract the life of our dreams, we have to learn to be conscious of our thoughts, not let them run away with us down paths that might affect our lives in detrimental ways.

Because wherever our attention is focused is where this energy goes. Mulford adds, 'Every thought … is something which goes to that person, thing or locality on which it is placed… Every thought represents an outlay of force…'

Not only that, but as New Thought writer Florence Scovel Shinn quotes from an alchemist and teacher in ancient Egypt, Hermes Trismegistus: 'All mental states were accompanied by vibrations. You combine with what you vibrate to, so let us all vibrate to success, happiness and abundance.'

'New' thoughts come from the light within you

But where do thoughts come from in the first place, and how can we use them to our advantage to attract the life we want? Mulford, and many others in the New Thought movement, believed that, 'The Supreme Wisdom, Power and Intelligence is in everything that exists from the atom to the planet. The Supreme Power and Wisdom is more than *in* everything. The Supreme Mind is every atom of the mountain, the sea, the tree, the bird, the animal, the man, the woman.'

Shinn calls this divine intelligence the 'superconscious mind'. She explains that there are 'three departments of the mind, the *subconscious*, *conscious* and *superconscious*. The subconscious is simply power without direction... it does what it is directed to do... Whatever man feels deeply or images clearly is impressed upon the subconscious mind and carried out in minutest detail. The conscious mind has been called the mortal or carnal mind. It is the human mind and sees life as it *appears to be*. It sees death, disaster, sickness, poverty and limitation of every kind, and it impresses the subconscious.

'The superconscious mind is the God Mind within each man, and is the realm of perfect ideas. In it is the *"perfect pattern"* spoken of by Plato, *The Divine Design*; for there is a *Divine Design* for each person. There is a perfect picture of this in the superconscious mind. It usually flashes across the conscious as an unattainable ideal – "something too good to be true". In reality, it is man's true destiny (or destination) flashed to him from the Infinite Intelligence which is *within himself*.'

The trick is to align your thoughts and desires with what this divine intelligence or the superconscious mind wants to manifest through you.

The law of attraction works when you tune into and resonate with this divinity, the Christ energy, inside you, sense what it holds for you and let it unfold. This is the 'New' aspect of New Thought: the 'truth' of God constantly revealing itself to the world, through each and every one of us.

To connect with this Christ light within us, we have to stop the frantic *doing* and distractions, and spend more time just *being*. We must still the chattering of the mind long enough to hear the prompts of our divine nature. Only when we are relaxed and calm can we receive from the superconscious mind and feel the deeper urges of divinity through our intuition. The best way to do this is through meditation.

HOW TO MEDITATE

Ten to 20 minutes of meditation is all you need to start with, increasing to half an hour or more, if you wish. You could set a gentle alarm for a certain time. But if it's on your phone, turn it to aeroplane mode so you are not interrupted by any calls or texts.

• Find a quiet, comfortable space to sit or kneel, either on cushions, on the floor or on a chair, as long as your spine is upright and you won't fidget. You could place a blanket on your legs, or a shawl on your shoulders, to stay warm.

• Settle down into a comfortable posture, back straight, chin slightly tucked in.

• Place your hands on your lap, with palms facing upwards in receiving mode.

• Softly close your eyes and start to become aware of your breath, breathing regularly in and out of your nose. Feel the air move in your nostrils with each breath.

(continued)

- Now start taking some longer, deeper breaths, really filling your lungs with fresh air, perhaps holding that in-breath for a few seconds, and then releasing that breath and again waiting a few seconds before drawing another breath in. Allow the breath to gently fall into its natural rhythm and let your whole body and mind relax.

- Become really present in your body, allowing any wandering thoughts to come and go, without getting caught up in any narrative in your mind. Try placing your awareness on your third-eye space, right between your eyebrows. This is the gateway to hearing, feeling and knowing your own inner wisdom, which is connected to the superconscious mind.

- You could try visualizing a column of bright white light flowing from the heavens into your crown chakra, on the top of your head, and down into your heart. Feel your heart expand with this light of consciousness as it connects you with the cosmos. Feel the bliss that bathing in this white light brings. Sit in this field of divinity for as long as you wish. If you sense any guidance via inspiration, visions or creative urges, note it down afterwards and act on it as soon as you can.

• When you are ready, thank the divine intelligence for revealing itself to you. Ground yourself by bringing your awareness back into your body and feeling the floor beneath you.

• Take your time going back to your day with a renewed awareness of the Christ light within you as it reveals itself, through you, in every moment.

Daily meditation practice, with its calm connection to the spirit within you, is an effective way to keep your vibration high. Spending more and more time living from a higher frequency means you are increasingly likely to attract scenarios that match your peaceful and elevated state of mind. You can meditate any time your thoughts start racing, slipping into old, negative thinking patterns, such as resentment, anger or ill-will. Just close your eyes, take a few deep breaths, and bring your awareness back to the present moment for a few minutes.

Stay present

Present-moment awareness, or mindfulness, is another practice to cultivate connection to Source, with the added benefit of bringing power and ease to your actions. Prentice Mulford found out as a boy in the California gold diggings, when an old-timer told him to 'put his mind into the shovel as well as his body.' He discovered that, 'Shovelling dirt needed cooperation of mind with muscle, mind to give direction to muscle; mind to place the shovel's point where it should scoop up most dirt with least outlay of strength... I found that the more thought I put in the shovel the better could I shovel: the less like work it became, the more like play it became, and the longer my strength for shovelling lasted. I found when my thought drifted on other things (no matter what), that soon the less strength and enjoyment had I for shovelling, and the sooner it became an irksome task.'

He was vastly ahead of his time in extolling the benefits of being mindful: 'You must drill your mind to put its whole thought on the act you are now doing. If you tie your shoe, think "shoe" and nothing else... sharpen a pencil for 60 consecutive seconds without thinking of something else ... If we can do this, we are possessed of a share of the greatest power in the universe, not only in making ourselves more happy, but also power for doing more of whatever we have to do, and doing it better and better.'

To be more mindful in every moment, start, again, by bringing your attention to your breathing, feeling each breath come into and go out of your body, via the nostrils or chest rising and falling. Focus on your body and your senses. Feel the sensation of the sun on your face, the fabric of your clothes, the grass under your feet. Hear all the sounds around you, such as birdsong or music. Really see what's in front of you, appreciating every detail, in your child or pet's face, a painting, your dinner. When eating or drinking, explore the smells, tastes and texture of every mouthful. Tuning deeply into your senses, with gratitude that you can, leads to an awareness that all is well in this present moment. There is no need to worry over the future or stress about the past if you can enjoy every moment with full awareness. Then, from that place of deep connectedness to and acceptance of *what is*, all good can unfold.

Fearful thinking dims our light

Meditation and mindfulness practices are essential to overcoming 'old' ways of thinking to allow the 'new' thoughts from the divinity within you to flourish. If we are not conscious of our thoughts, it's easy to get stuck in old habits of negative thinking. Ruminating over past events, criticizing others, feeling jealousy, doubt and anxiety, or fearful fretting over the future are all techniques of the ego trying to keep us safe from perceived harm. These habitual thought programmes may come from past experiences, but such thinking blocks the light of consciousness within us. If we want to evolve as humans, be the best versions of ourselves and manifest our dream lives, we have to release fear-based thoughts and limiting beliefs so we can truly radiate our Christ-light into the world.

Florence Shinn declares that 'Nothing stands between man[1] and his highest ideals and every desire of his heart but doubt and fear. When man can "wish without worrying" every desire will be instantly fulfilled ... Fear must be erased from the consciousness – it is man's only enemy – fear of lack, fear of failure, fear of sickness, fear of loss and a

---

1 When any original New Thought writer of a bygone era, such as Shinn, Mulford and others, say 'he', 'him' and 'man', they mean 'mankind', as in 'humankind' and not man as opposed to woman.

feeling of insecurity on some plane …Jesus Christ said, "Why are ye fearful, oh ye of little faith?" Matthew 8.26. We can see we must substitute faith for fear, for fear is only inverted faith.'

As Shinn says, we must cultivate faith that if something is part of the divine plan for us, it will manifest. She firmly believes, 'Infinite intelligence is ever ready to carry out man's smallest or greatest demands,' as long as they are part of the divine plan. We have to trust in the Universal Consciousness that our righteous desires will come into being – not always in the way we may have imagined, but in the way that is part of the divine design for our life.

Thoughts affect our health

Perpetual negative-thinking habits can seriously affect not only our mental wellbeing but our physical health as well. According to many New Thought teachers, as well as more recent self-help writers, our state of mind directly affects the health of our body. Louise Hay's first book, *You Can Heal Your Life*, included a long directory of all bodily afflictions caused by 'wrong' thinking. Shinn's writing in the 1920s also explored this connection: 'The metaphysician knows that all disease has a mental correspondence, and in order to heal the body one must first "heal the soul". The soul is the subconscious mind, and it must be "saved" from wrong thinking.

'Continual criticism produces rheumatism, as critical inharmonious thoughts cause unnatural deposits in the blood, which settle in the joints. False growths are caused by jealousy, hatred, unforgiveness, fear etc. Every disease is caused by a mind not at ease. Unforgiveness is the most prolific cause of disease. It will harden arteries or liver, and affect eye-sight. In its train are endless ills,' she says.

Shinn firmly believed that 'All sickness and unhappiness come from the violation of the law of love...Many people have attracted disease and unhappiness through condemnation of others. What a

man condemns in others, he attracts to himself.' But, she adds, 'The body may be renewed and transformed through the spoken word and clear vision, and disease completely wiped out of the consciousness.'

Relationships depend on how we think

If we continually think a certain way, it shapes our appearance, which in turn affects how others see us. As Mulford explains, 'The prevailing state of mind, or character of thought, shapes the body and features. It makes us ugly or pleasing, attractive or repulsive to others. Our thought shapes our gestures, our mannerism, our walk. Look at the discontented, gloomy, melancholy, and ill-tempered men or women, and you see in their faces proof of the action of this silent force of their unpleasant thought, cutting, carving, and shaping them to their present expression. Such people are never in good health, for that force acts on them as poison, and creates some form of disease.'

When someone is appealing, we say they are magnetic. Mulford says, 'Magnetic power or influence is simply thought felt by others. If your thought is despondent, gloomy, jealous, carping, cynical, it repels. If cheerful, hopeful, and full of earnest desire to do the most good possible to any one you meet... it attracts...It is an element felt pleasantly or unpleasantly by others, inspiring them with confidence or distrust.'

Whatever energy you emit can be felt by others, whether near or far away – and it often comes back to you in some way. Says Mulford, 'Every disorderly meeting, every family quarrel, every discordance... sends into the air a wave of destructive and unpleasant substance.' As an act of self-preservation, we must strive, Mulford advises, 'to forget enemies, or to throw out to them only friendly thought... The persistent thought of friendliness turns aside thought of ill-will, and renders it harmless. The injunction of Christ to do good to your enemies is founded on a natural law. It is saying that the thought or element of good-will carries the greater power, and will always turn aside and prevent injury from the thought of ill-will.'

Even when fighting with others, remember they too are Christ-consciousness in human form. Shinn says we must state, '*Every man is a golden link in the chain of my good.* For all men are God in manifestation, awaiting the opportunity given by man, himself, to serve the divine plan of his life. Bless your enemy, and you rob him of his ammunition – this law is true of nations as well as individuals. Bless a nation, send love and good-will to every inhabitant and it is robbed of its power to harm.'

The power in sending goodwill to those we don't get on with or who stand in the way of our success diffuses their hold over us, protecting us, too. Says Shinn, 'If you are centred and send out only good-will to others, you cannot be touched or influenced by any negative thoughts of others...Good-will produces a great aura of protection about the one who sends it.'

Forgiving and thinking loving thoughts towards all other humans, regardless of how they may have treated us, is far better for your health and wellbeing than holding onto any anger or hatred. Plus, letting go of any negativity frees us to focus on more positive and productive activities.

Fear and worry harm our children

Thoughts of worry are also harmful. With the 'wasted energy' of worry, as Mulford calls it, you lose strength of the mind, and, 'When it frets, it sends out force to the thing fretted about. These states of mind, acts of thought, and useless waste of force become at last so confirmed in habit, that the spirit may lose all power of bringing all its strength together.'

It's a common habit for parents, especially, to constantly worry about their children. It may seem perfectly natural and understandable, given the amount of dangers that can befall them, yet it can attract the situation being worried about. Shinn explains, 'A friend asked a woman if her little girl had had the measles yet. She replied promptly, "Not yet!" This implied that she was expecting the illness, and, therefore, preparing the way for what she did not want for herself and child.'

Children are sensitive and receptive to what others think about them. Parents should not continually hold thoughts of fear about their offspring and watch for issues to unfold. Send only goodwill to your sons and daughters and trust in the divine intelligence within them to keep them safe, lead them on their divine path and attract only the best for them.

Furthermore, adds Shinn, 'Parents should never force careers or professions upon their children.' Before they are born, and whenever you find yourself stressing about their direction, state the following:

'Let the God in this child have perfect expression; let the Divine Design of his [or her] mind, body and affairs be made manifest throughout his [or her] life, throughout eternity.'

So much begins and ends with our thoughts. We must choose them wisely rather than letting them roam wildly, in a harmful way to mental and physical health, causing obstacles to total bliss and fulfilment. Then, when you are aware of your thinking and can consciously direct it from the expansive light within you, anything is possible.

CHAPTER 2

POSITIVE
WORDS

The right words, spoken out loud or in your head, have the power to amplify positive thoughts and totally transform your life. It's essential to be conscious of what you are saying, both to yourself and to others, and speak with integrity and kindness. Not only is this a key tenet of the New Thought ideology, but 'Be impeccable with your word' is the first of the Toltec tradition's Four Agreements shared by Don Miguel Ruiz. Ruiz guides us to say what we actually mean, with directness and awareness, never gossip about people, and use the power of our words in the direction of love and truth. The law of attraction demands the same: ask for what you want correctly and universal intelligence will provide. Or, as the Bible states, 'Ask and ye shall receive.' Spoken phrases, or affirmations, act like spells to bring about what is being declared, especially if said regularly enough and with the full force of your beliefs behind them.

Ask correctly and it is given

In *The Game of Life and How to Play It*, Florence
Scovel Shinn says, 'There is nothing too great of an
accomplishment for the man who knows the power
of his word, and who follows his intuitive leads.
By the word, he starts in action unseen forces and
can rebuild his body or remould his affairs.' In fact,
she continues, 'You can change your conditions
by changing your words, impressing upon your
subconscious mind what you would like to happen as
if it were already done.'

Quantum physics today has proven the existence
of the quantum field, where everything exists all at
once and can influence every moment in any way we
choose. This ties in with the New Thought belief in
the great one-ness of everything, where all life and
its manifestations are part of the same Source energy
or divine intelligence, and everything that is still to
come is in fact already manifested in the divine mind.
Past and future are man-made constructs; in actuality
there is only this ever-expanding present moment,
where all you desire is on its way to you. You just have
to get into alignment with it to attract it.

As Shinn explains, 'All the good that is to be made
manifest in man's life is already an accomplished fact
in divine mind, and is released through recognition,
or spoken word, so he must be careful to decree

that only the Divine Idea be made manifest, for often he decrees, through his "idle words", failure or misfortune.'

It is essential to word your demands correctly by always asking for the 'divine selection' or for whatever you want to be part of the 'divine plan'. If, for example, financial abundance is what you'd like, you can state the following often, as suggested by Shinn:

'Infinite Spirit, open the way
for my immediate supply,
let all that is mine by divine
right now reach me, in great
avalanches of abundance.'

You can then ask for a direction to go in to receive this abundance, by saying,

'Give me a definite lead,

let me know if there is

anything for me to do.'

Then see what comes to mind, or what signs or leads present themselves through ideas, inspiration or creative urges (more on this in the next chapter, on intuition).

Similarly, Shinn recommends stating,

'Infinite Spirit, open the way

for my right home, my right

friend, my right position. I give

thanks as it now manifests

under grace, in a perfect way.'

She adds, 'The latter part of this sentence is most important,' to avoid things coming to you but out of some misfortune instead.

So, for **financial abundance** you can state any of the following affirmations from Shinn's book *Your Word Is Your Wand*:

'My supply comes from God and big, happy, financial surprises now come to me, under grace, in perfect ways!'

'Infinite Spirit, open the
way for my great abundance.
I am an irresistible magnet
for all that belongs to me by
Divine Right.'

'I now release the gold-mine
within me. I am linked with
an endless golden stream
of prosperity, which comes to
me under grace, in
perfect ways.'

'All that is now mine by
Divine Right is now
released and reaches me
in great avalanches of
abundance, under grace in
miraculous ways.'

'My supply is endless,
inexhaustible and immediate,
and comes to me under grace
in perfect ways.'

'I spend money under direct inspiration, wisely and fearlessly, knowing my supply is endless and immediate.'

Words to bring real change

If you're feeling especially brave or in need of change, Shinn suggests saying:

'Infinite Spirit, open the way for the Divine Design of my life to manifest; let the genius within me now be released. Let me see clearly the perfect plan.'

However, she adds, 'When one has made this demand, he may find great changes taking place in his life, for nearly every man has wandered far from the Divine Design.'

We may be following a path to please or appease others, or doing things more out of fear or anxiety about what others may think. We worry we may not be successful in a certain career, or might shock people with our choice of partner, for example, if we go for what we truly want. We might fear losing all our money if we take a huge financial risk on the path of our dreams, or play it small with our desires out of fear of failure. But this is all habitual negative thinking, often based on past experience, such as trauma or parental programming, or sometimes unfounded irrational fears of change. It all comes from the subconscious mind and needs to be 're-programmed' by our new words and actions. Plus, we have to connect with the superconscious mind, the Christ consciousness within us, and let that lead the way.

Similarly strong and powerful statements to shift your life into alignment with Source energy, also from Shinn, are:

'The genius within me is now released. I now fulfil my destiny.'

'The Divine Design of my life now comes to pass. I now fill the place that I can fill and no one else can fill. I now do the things which I can do and no one else can do.'

'All doors now open for happy surprises and the Divine Plan of my life is speeded up under grace.'

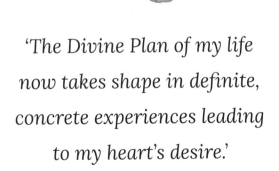

'I now see clearly the perfect plan of my life. Divine enthusiasm fires me up and I now fulfil my destiny.'

'The Divine Plan of my life now takes shape in definite, concrete experiences leading to my heart's desire.'

Shinn calls fear-based thoughts 'burdens'. She explains: 'A burden is an adverse thought or condition, and this thought or condition has its root in the subconscious. It seems almost impossible to make any headway directing the subconscious from the conscious, or reasoning, mind, as the reasoning mind (the intellect) is limited in its conceptions, and filled with doubts and fears. [Instead] cast the burden upon the superconscious mind (or Christ within) where it is "made light" or dissolved into its "native nothingness".

'For example, a woman in urgent need of money, made ... the statement,

"I cast the burden of lack on the Christ within and I go free to have plenty!"

The belief in lack was her burden and as she cast it upon the superconscious with its belief of plenty, an avalanche of [financial] supply was the result.'

Shinn explains further, 'I have noticed, in "casting the burden", after a little while one seems to see clearly. It is impossible to have clear vision, while in the throes of the carnal mind. Doubts and fears poison the mind and body, and imagination runs riot, attracting disaster and disease. In steadily repeating the affirmation,"*I cast this burden on the Christ within, and go free,*" the vision clears, and with it [comes] a feeling of relief, and sooner or later comes the manifestation of good, be it health, happiness or supply.'

Another woman Shinn knew had the burden of resentment. 'She said, "*I cast this burden of resentment on the Christ within, and I go free, to be loving, harmonious and happy.*" The Almighty superconscious flooded the subconscious with love, and her whole life was changed. For years, resentment had held her in a state of torment and imprisoned her soul (the subconscious mind).'

Try these affirmations from Shinn to dissolve your burdens of fear, resentment, jealousy or lack, and flood your consciousness with the loving energy of the universe:

'I put this situation in the hands of Infinite Love and Wisdom. If this is the Divine plan, I bless it and no longer resist, but if it is not divinely planned, I give thanks now that it is now dissolved and dissipated.'

'Divine Love now dissolves
and dissipates every wrong
condition in my mind, body
and affairs. Divine Love is
the most powerful chemical
in the universe, and dissolves
everything which is not
of itself.'

'Divine Love floods my
consciousness with health,
and every cell in my body is
filled with light.'

'The Light of Christ within
now wipes out all fear, doubt,
anger and resentment. God's
love pours through me, an
irresistible magnetic current.'

Shinn adds, 'If you still have any relentless fearful thoughts or beliefs in your subconscious, state the following:

"I now smash and demolish(by my spoken word) every untrue record in my subconscious mind. They shall return to the dust-heap of their native nothingness, for they came from my own vain imaginings. I now make perfect my record through the Christ within – the record of health, wealth, love and perfect self-expression."

These four aspects of life Shinn calls 'the square of life', the fulfilment of which, 'brings perfect happiness'. It is these areas of health, wealth, love and perfect self-expression that this book helps you attract, as who doesn't want to manifest the very best this 'square of life' has to offer?

Start the day with the right words

Many of us start the day going through a list of jobs to do, ruminating on the events of the past and worrying about what's to come. But as New Thought writer Ralph Waldo Trine said, 'To get up each morning with the resolve to be happy, is to condition circumstances instead of being conditioned by them.'

Using the power of the spoken word to help things go well is a principle shared by Jesus Christ, and explained by Shinn: 'Man's word is his wand filled with magic and power! Jesus Christ emphasised the power of the word... saying, 'death and life are in the power of the tongue.' So man has the power to change an unhappy condition by waving over it the wand of his word.'

Try saying some of the following statements from Shinn as you rise from slumber, to set yourself up for a day of success:

'Today is a day of completion; I give thanks for this perfect day, miracle shall follow miracle and wonders shall never cease.'

'I look with wonder at that
which is before me.'

'Now is the appointed time.
Today is the day of my
amazing good fortune.'

'Endless good now comes to
me in endless ways.'

'My supply comes from God,
and big, happy financial
surprises now come to me,
under grace, in perfect ways.'

These simple sayings also set the tone for the day:

Today is a wonderful day.
I allow my soul to lead
the way and I am open to
exciting opportunities.

I start my day with positivity
and appreciation, receptive
to new experiences.

I allow the Universe to flow
through me today.

My day unfolds with ease,
joy and fulfilment.

All is well and I am right
where I am meant to be.

Make saying affirmations a habit every morning and you shall see wonders, miracles and good fortune come your way as the subconscious starts to be re-programmed to accept all you desire. Shinn says, 'Continually affirming establishes the belief in the subconscious... One should not plead... but give thanks repeatedly, that he has received.'

It's from a state of gratitude for everything in our lives, good or bad, happening or still to come, that better situations and experiences unfold. Try these affirmations giving thanks, from Shinn's *Your Word is Your Wand*, or create your own, depending on what you want to attract:

'I give thanks for my whirlwind success. I sweep all before me for I work with the Spirit and follow the Divine Plan of my life.'

'I give thanks that the millions which are mine by Divine Right now pour in and pile up under grace in perfect ways.'

'I give thanks for my permanent happiness, my permanent health, my permanent wealth, my permanent love.'

Whatever affirmation you use to start your day, or to keep your thoughts elevated throughout your week, it must ring true for you. Any doubt about what you're saying negates the power of the words and won't have as magnetic a power of attraction. As Shinn says, 'One should never use an affirmation unless it is absolutely satisfying and convincing to his own consciousness.'

Tweak any affirmation so it resonates more with you to suit your own circumstances. Always keep it upbeat, and state what it is you want to attract as if it is already manifest, asking divine intelligence to bring whatever is yours 'by divine right' to you. 'The divine pattern is the only safe pattern to work by,' says Shinn. 'Man should only demand that which is his *by divine right.*'

For example:

> *'Infinite Intelligence, give me the right house [or car/relationship/ sofa etc] equally as charming as this... which is mine by divine right.'*

'I am now linked by an invisible, unbreakable magnetic cord with all that belongs to me by Divine Right.'

'I let go of everything not divinely designed for me, and the perfect plan of my life now comes to pass.'

'The Divine Plan of my life
cannot be tampered with.
It is incorruptible and
indestructible. It awaits only
my recognition.'

Shinn recommends the following as a successful
affirmation to attract the right work:

'I have wonderful work,
in a wonderful way, I give
wonderful service, for
wonderful pay.'

She explains, 'It makes a most powerful statement as there should always be perfect payment for perfect service, and a rhyme links easily into the subconscious.'

One of her clients dances to music and sings her affirmations every morning. Shinn explains, 'The rhythm and harmony of music and motion carry her words forth with tremendous power.'

Even as far back as the early 1900s, New Thought writers such as Shinn were talking about humans raising their frequency to higher dimensions: 'Music has a fourth dimensional quality and releases the soul from imprisonment. It makes wonderful things seem possible, and easy [to accomplish]...Playing music puts you in perfect harmony and releases the imagination.'

Singing your affirmations to musical accompaniment is a great way to raise your energy, as dancing and singing always do. It makes saying your affirmations extra joyful and high-vibe, which is key to imprinting them upon the subconscious mind and helping them manifest.

Whatever affirmation you choose, says Shinn, 'The statement should be made over and over and over, sometimes for hours at a time, silently or audibly, with quietness or determination. We must wind ourselves up with spoken words.'

You might want to add some positive statements after a time spent meditating in the morning. Say them while looking deeply into your eyes in the mirror to give them more power. Or write them on post-it notes placed around your home to remind you to say each statement when you see it. You could even repeat these powerful phrases before you go to sleep, as a form of prayer, thanking the Almighty Power for all you desire, whether it's more happiness, a deeper love or perfect health. Here are some more affirmations from Shinn:

For more happiness

'I have a wonderful joy
in a wonderful way,
and my wonderful joy
has come to stay.'

'Happy surprises come to me
each day.'

'I am harmonious, happy,
radiant: detached from the
tyranny of fear. '

'My good now flows to me
in a steady, unbroken, ever-
increasing stream of happiness.'

'As I am one with God I am now
one with my heart's desire.'

'I am harmonious, happy and
Divinely magnetic, and now
draw to me all God's ideas
for me, which are perfect and
permanent.'

For perfect health

'I am a spiritual being – my body is perfect, made in his likeness and image. The Light of Christ now streams through every cell. I give thanks for my radiant health.'

'I am nourished by the spirit within. Every cell of my body is filled with light. I give thanks for radiant health and endless happiness.'

'The Light of Christ now
floods my consciousness,
dissolving acid thoughts. I
love everyone and everyone
loves me. I give thanks for
my radiant health and
happiness.'

For deep love

'I love everyone and everyone
loves me. My apparent enemy
becomes my friend, a golden
link in the chain of my good.'

'I am at peace with myself
and with the whole world. I
love everyone and everyone
loves me.'

'I forgive everyone and
everyone forgives me.
The gates swing open for
my good.'

'My good now overtakes me
in a surprising way.'

CHAPTER 3

ACTING ON INTUITION

Learning to tune into your intuition and acting on that guidance is essential with the law of attraction. But what exactly is 'intuition' and how do we know it's the truth? *In-tuition* literally means tuition from within. As Prentice Mulford says, 'Intuition means the inward teaching, and the inward teacher. This teacher resides in all of you. Give it free play, and demand also of the infinite Spirit wisdom, guidance, and suggestion, and it will grow into genius.'

It's the part of the superconscious mind inside you; the consciousness behind all thoughts, words and actions; the peaceful stillness that connects everything and from which all life unfolds. The more you quiet your thoughts through meditation or mindfulness practices, the easier it is to tune into your internal guidance.

Connecting to this awareness inside you just takes a little discipline, determination and practice.

Religions have always used mantras and prayer to calm and focus the mind, and connect to a deeper state of peace inside. Chanting sacred sounds or repeating meaningful words opens the channel to God, the Universe, your divine path. Simply chanting 'om' three times and then listening to the stillness afterwards can tune you into the universal energy within. Do this daily and you start to go deeper and feel the teachings from within get stronger and louder.

From this place of peace and deep connectedness, really listen to your body and be aware of all your feelings as and when they arise. This helps you get a clearer sense of what your inner awareness is telling you. Often, intuition is felt in the tummy, hence the phrase 'gut feeling'. But it could come more as a sense of being pulled in a certain direction. Think of it as an internal compass pointing you on the right path to your highest expression by giving you creative impulses, desires and goals you'd like to achieve. It's the sense that you have to do something, go somewhere or connect with someone, however unusual that urge might be.

In her book *The Power of the Spoken Word*, Shinn explains the power of our intuitive hunches: 'Intuition is a spiritual faculty above the intellect. It is the "still small voice" [as the Bible calls it] commonly called a

hunch, which says "This is the way, walk ye in it"...it is the most important part of spiritual development. It is Divine Guidance, the God within.

'Intuition always looks after our interests,' she continues. 'Intuition is our unerring guide. Practise following it in the little things, then you will learn to trust it in big things. I have a friend who is very intuitive. She sometimes calls up and says, "I've just had a hunch to call you up so I thought I would find out what it is about." Invariably I have some mission for her.'

So let your intuition tell you what to eat and drink, what to read or watch, and see where it leads. Give it a choice between two things and sense which one gives you the strongest impulse to choose it. Out on a walk, ask yourself which direction to go and allow your inner wisdom to guide you. It's usually the first choice you make, or the one that feels the most right. Like Shinn's friend, if you get a sudden urge to call someone, do it. Or if you keep thinking about going

somewhere or doing something, even if not what you'd normally do, follow the guidance and go for it!

More often than not, when you follow your intuitive impulses everything works out well or at least teaches you something more about yourself and leads you on to the next part of your journey. As spiritual teacher Lorie Ladd, who brings New Thought up to date for today, says, 'Everything is moving me into the next highest version of myself.' So following our internal guidance usually means things align to work in your favour. When you take one step in the direction of your intuitive urges, infinite wisdom comes to meet you. Then synchronicity occurs and you find yourself in the right place at the right time, receiving the right information, fully in the natural flow of universal energy.

However, it's not always easy to follow intuition. After years of ignoring or denying it, or always using the rational mind to work things out, it takes practice to hear and act on our hunches. As Shinn says, 'To work with God-power, you must give it right of way and still the reasoning mind. The instant you ask, Infinite Intelligence knows the way to fulfilment... Infinite Intelligence knows the way out. Infinite Intelligence knows where the supply is for every demand. But we must trust it, keep our poise, and give it right of way...It is very difficult for the average person to "stand still", which means keep your poise, and let Infinite Intelligence run the situation.'

Plus, it's not necessarily the easiest path, and there will of course be hard work and challenges, because that's life too. But a life led by intuition is your soul and divine spirit showing you the way, urging you to be more, share more, grow more. You just have to listen deeply to the answers to your questions, follow the signs of the superconscious mind, and trust in the divinity within you to show you the way.

American writer, mystic and medical intuitive Caroline Myss explains how you know it's intuition as opposed to make-believe: 'Intuition makes you feel uncomfortable, whereas fantasy doesn't. It's that kind of funky feeling when you meet someone and you

think, "I've got to get to know that person," but you don't know why. But with clear intuition there comes a package of courage that you don't get with fantasy. This package of strength that you get is like a little battery that gets plugged into your gut and it begins to throb constantly until you start doing something about it. When you start following it, you begin to experience the phenomenon of synchronicity.'

As you start to trust in the power of your intuition to lead you in the right direction, you align more with your divine path as it manifests, often in a magical way. As Shinn writes: 'As you believe in yourself and the God-power within, fear and anxiety drop away. You establish the vibration of assurance. This is true of an intuitive person. Every move is made under divine guidance and he never violates a "hunch", therefore he is always in the right place at the right time. However, it often takes great courage to follow intuition. It takes a Viking, who is unafraid, to sail in unknown seas.'

She adds, 'We have the power of choice – we may follow the magic path of intuition, or the long hard road of experience, by following the reasoning mind. By following the superconscious we attain the heights. The superconscious is the realm of inspiration, revelation, illumination and intuition. Inspiration (which is divine guidance) is the most important thing in life. The superconscious is the realm of perfect ideas. The great genius captures his thoughts from the superconscious.'

Yet even when well tuned into your internal guidance, you still might not be sure of the right choice, especially when faced with a tough decision. Shinn insists that, 'No matter what you are doing, ask for guidance. It saves time, energy and often a lifetime of misery. All suffering comes from the violation of intuition. Get into the *habit of hunching*, then you will always be on the magic path.'

In order to overcome indecision, Shinn
recommends that we 'Make the statement repeatedly,

"I am always under direct inspiration: I make right decisions quickly."

These words impress the subconscious, and soon
one finds himself awake and alert, making his right
moves without hesitation.'

Furthermore, Shinn says, you can 'Ask for a
definite lead, and you will receive it,' adding that
'Every day there is a necessity of choice (a fork in the
road). "Shall I do this, or shall I do that? Shall I stay,
or shall I go?" Many people do not know what to do...
The intuitive person is never undecided: he is given
leads and hunches and goes boldly ahead, knowing
he is on the magic path... always ask for definite leads
just what to do; you will always receive one if you ask
for it. Sometimes it comes as an intuition, sometimes
from the external.'

External signs can be anything you spot in answer
to your query, from a billboard poster or vehicle
advertisement to an overheard conversation, such
as this one that Shinn shares: 'One of my students,

named Ada, was walking down the street, undecided whether to go to a certain place, or not; she asked for a lead. Two women were walking in front of her. One turned to the other and said, "Why don't you go, Ada?" The woman's name just happened to be Ada – my friend took it as a definite lead, and went on to her destination, and the outcome was very successful.

'We really lead magic lives, guided and provided for at every step: if we have ears to hear and eyes that see,' says Shinn. 'Of course, we have left the plane of intellect and are drawing from the superconscious, the God within, which says, "This is the way, walk ye in it." Whatever you should know, will be revealed to you. Whatever you lack, will be provided. [But] you must live in the now and be wide awake to your opportunities.'

Focusing the mind on the present

Living in the now means being aware of every moment, tuning into your deeper wisdom in the present so you can pick up on its guidance every step of the way. You must not be continually ruminating over the past or worrying over the future. These unnecessary mental habits will block the connection to your intuition; they stir up strong feelings that get in the way of the benevolent universal flow of energy.

When you catch your mind racing in one direction or another, stop, take a few deep breaths and simply drop into the now by being aware of everything you can sense in this present moment. It may be the birds singing, the breeze on your face, your body sitting on the chair or the noise of a clock ticking. Feel your breath entering your nostrils, expanding your chest, filling your lungs. State all the things you are aware of right now, and your awareness of the present moment will grow.

Shinn clarifies how we can connect more clearly to God consciousness: 'Prayer is telephoning to God and intuition is God telephoning to you. Many people have a "busy wire" when God telephones and they don't get the message. Your wire is busy when you get discouraged, angry or resentful. You've heard the expression "I was so mad I couldn't see straight." We might add, "I was so mad I couldn't hear straight."

Your negative emotions drown out the voice of intuition.

'We must stop planning, plotting and scheming and let Infinite Intelligence solve the problem in its own way,' she says. 'God-power is subtle, silent and irresistible ... Some people are naturally intuitive and are always in contact with Universal Intelligence, but by taking an affirmation we make a conscious contact.'

Affirmations to focus on your intuition and the good coming your way include any of the following from Shinn's work, or you can create your own.

'Divine Intelligence, reveal to me the way.'

'Infinite
Spirit, reveal
to me the way,
let me know
what I am to
do next.'

'I am divinely sensitive to
my intuitive leads and give
instant obedience to Thy will.'

'I am harmonious, poised and magnetic. My power is God's power and it is irresistible.'

'Divine order is now established in my mind, body and affairs. I see clearly and act quickly and my greatest expectations come to pass in miraculous ways.'

'Never argue with a hunch.'

Relax and rest to really hear your intuition

You cannot force intuition. It is a natural phenomenon that needs time to come from within and be received by you. The best way to sense it is to relax and rest from the hustle and bustle of daily activity and distractions.

Prentice Mulford explains, 'The more free the mind is left to follow its own teaching, its intuition, the guidance of the spirit, the greater the inspiration... The mood of repose, of unruffled and serene mind, is the mood in which all manner of discoveries are made, and ideas grasped or received. The name of the person temporarily escaped from memory rarely comes when we are "trying hard" to think of it. It is only when we cease trying to think, that the name comes to us. Indeed, this trying to think causes an unconscious straining of muscle. We try to work our brains. We send the blood to the head in this effort. All this is an obstacle to the spirit.'

A relaxed state is best to be successful in business especially, says Mulford: 'The profit of not over-working or over-straining the body is proven all about us in the everyday affairs of life. The most successful man in business is he of the coolest head, the self-contained man, who has intuitively learned to keep his body free from fatigue, so that his spirit can work.'

Shinn agrees: 'Your big opportunity and big success usually slide in when you least expect it. You have to let go long enough for the great law of attraction to operate. You never saw a worried and anxious magnet. It stands up straight and hasn't a care in the world, because it knows the needles can't help jumping to it. The things we rightly desire come to pass when we have taken the clutch off... You are completely demagnetized when you desire something too intensely.'

Both share examples of how being relaxed, calm and self-contained attract all good things to you, via following your intuitive hunches, as you are not stressing and struggling to reach your goals but allowing them to be attracted to you naturally. In a relaxed state, you are more likely to come up with new ideas, better plans, and to sense your inner wisdom as it urges you forward on your divine path.

Mulford calls it being led by spirit, suggesting that, 'If you have lost your way, you will find it much quicker by going very slowly, so keeping the spirit concentrated, instead of rushing the body about hither and thither, without aim or object. The experienced hunter puts himself in this frame of mind, and saunters through the woods; while the ignorant city boy, wild with excitement, rushes over miles of territory and sees no game. In both these cases, when the body is made to a degree apathetic, does a certain power, an unrecognized sense, go out and find for you your way.'

He describes the best relaxed state as when, 'You find yourself, without knowing why, in the self-contained, satisfied, contented mood of spirit. You are able to walk leisurely. You are in no hurry. No wild or unconquerable desire is upon you. You feel at peace with all the world. You have forgotten your enemies, your cares, your anxieties. It is then you most enjoy the woods, the skies, the passing crowd about you. It is in this mood that the spirit becomes as a magnet...drawing to you ideas...new plans, schemes, and inventions; you are sharpening all your faculties for any kind of work or business. Your spirit, so massed, is a power. When you are free from... anxiety, your real power has opportunity to act. That is the power of the spirit.'

Despite contemporary culture saying we always need to be busy and productive or entertained and distracted, the best way to attract all your desire is to take more time to rest and enjoy yourself. Mulford explains why: 'If you will give your body all the rest it needs, your mental force will work far and near more powerfully for you. Your plans will be deeper, and, when carried out, more productive of results. If the body is always fagged out, much of the force of that spirit must be used up in keeping a hold on the body, in other words, keeping it alive. It matters not whether you tire yourself out voluntarily, or are obliged to do so to get a living. The result is the same.'

It's a refreshing viewpoint now, let alone at the time he was writing, but Mulford fully endorses taking more time to enjoy yourself. He writes, 'When your opportunity comes, granting you four or five more hours daily of leisure, do not pile on yourself any extra effort for the sake of the few dollars you may get by it. This opportunity may be your first step out into a newer life. Give yourself leisure. Don't be afraid of enjoying yourself.'

It is by enjoying yourself, resting and relaxing into every moment that intuitive hunches will present themselves more and more. When they do, you will be well-rested enough to act on them as soon as you can, to allow your magic path to manifest in all its wondrous glory.

CHAPTER 4

ACTING ON INTENTIONS

It's not only thoughts and words that create your reality. Acting on your intentions is the next essential step to attracting all you desire. Many law of attraction experts say the key here is acting quickly, as soon as you have the urge or inspiration to do something that will take you one step closer to your goal. Even the smallest action towards your desires focuses energy in that direction and lets the universe know you mean business.

Write down exactly what you want: a new, more spacious home, a loving partner or an exciting and well-paid job. Then make a list of all the ideas you have to help bring this into your life. Step one might be doing a bit of research online or joining a dating site, for example. Once you do something, however simple or small, in the direction of your intentions, the next action will arise through your urges or inspirations, or simply be the next logical step to take. Follow the excitement you feel about the new thing coming into your life, always try to do the most fun option, and expect signs and synchronicities to show you the way forward. As spiritual writer and teacher Deepak Chopra says, 'An intention synchronistically organises its own fulfilment.'

If you hit an obstacle or a problem, don't let it deflate your positivity. Know that, as Shinn says often in her books, 'Nearly every big success is built upon a failure.' Act without worry of failing, as failure is merely a stepping stone to success, and may not be as bad as you fear. It's the fear of it that gets in the way of you attracting all that is rightfully yours according to your divine path. Plus, focusing on your fears can bring them into reality. So stay strong in your belief that you will succeed and let nothing deter you from your goal.

Mulford explains the strength in making an intention to stick to your purpose: 'There is a spiritual power or gift, which, when you have formed a plan or purpose in your mind, causes you to hold to it and not be led, swayed, influenced, cajoled, tempted, jeered, or ridiculed out of it by others. If you have resolved to be something, in art or business, greater and higher than you now seem to others, it will keep you to that resolve. The man or woman who succeeds must always in mind or imagination live, move, think, and act as if they had gained that success, or they never will gain it.'

According to the law of attraction, the energy of determination to succeed, of holding that intention clear in your mind, attracts the success you desire. It helps you get over any difficulties that may arise, seeing them as part of the path to your dreams. By keeping an awareness of this you can trust that everything that is meant for you is coming to you, in perfect timing.

Active faith

To show your trust and belief in all good manifesting for you, you must prepare for your blessings as if they are already here, even when there is no sight of them. Shinn calls it 'digging your ditches', after the Bible story of the three kings asking the prophet Elisha

for water, and he told them, 'Ye shall not see wind, neither shall ye see rain, yet make this valley full of ditches.' Prepare for the thing you have asked for and, like the three kings' ditches that were filled to overflowing with rain, your gifts will come.

Acting in good faith that your dreams will manifest impresses upon the subconscious mind that it is happening, and so it does because the subconscious doesn't know if a thing is real or imagined. Shinn goes on to explain, 'Faith is expectancy, [as the Bible says] "According to your faith, be it unto you."'

So expect the best, not the worst, by acting in any way that demonstrates your happy, fulfilling and abundant life is on its way. For example, if you want a new relationship in your life, you could set a place at the table or clear out clothes in a drawer for them to fill with their belongings when they move in with you. Or, says Shinn, 'If you have declared you would like a new home, prepare for it immediately by buying new ornaments or furniture for it.'

Shinn writes about her many clients who demonstrated this active faith and got exactly what they wanted. She says, 'I knew a woman who made the giant swing into faith, by buying a large arm-chair... for she was preparing for the right man. He came.'

Another woman wanted a new apartment and, even though there was a shortage, was certain she'd get one. Says Shinn, 'She spoke the words *Infinite Spirit, open the way for the right apartment...* She had contemplated buying new blankets, when... the adverse thought or reasoning mind suggested, "Don't buy the blankets, perhaps, after all, you won't get an apartment and you will have no use for them," She promptly replied (to herself), "I'll dig my ditches by buying the blankets!" So she prepared for the apartment – acted as though she already had it. She found one in a miraculous way, and it was given to her although there were over 200 other applicants. The blankets showed active faith.'

In the same vein, she explains, 'Many people are in ignorance of the fact that gifts and things are investments, and hoarding and saving inevitably leads to loss.'

She explains, 'I knew a man who wanted to buy a fur-lined overcoat. He and his wife went into various shops, but there was none he wanted. He said they were all too cheap-looking. At last, he was shown one the salesman said was valued at $1,000, but which the manager would sell him for $500, as it was late in the season. His financial possessions amounted to about $700. The reasoning mind would have said, "You can't afford to spend nearly all you have on a coat," but he was very intuitive and never reasoned. He turned to his wife and said, "If I get this coat, I'll make a ton of money!" So his wife consented, weakly. About a month later, he received a $10,000 commission. The coat made him feel so rich, it linked him with success and prosperity; without the coat, he would not have received the commission. It was an investment paying large dividends.'

Shinn urges us to remember, 'Man's supply is inexhaustible and unfailing when fully trusted, but faith or trust must precede the demonstration [of abundance].'

Giving is receiving

It is well known that different religions give, or *tithe*, a percentage of their income to their church or to charitable projects with the above principle in mind. As Shinn says, 'Giving opens the way for receiving. In order to create activity in one's finances, one should give. Tithing or giving one-tenth of one's income is an old Jewish custom, and is sure to bring increase. Many of the richest men in this country [the United States] have been tithers, and I have never known it to fail as an investment. The tenth-part goes forth and returns blessed and multiplied. But the gift, or tithe, must be given with love and cheerfulness, for "God loveth a cheerful giver." Bills should be paid cheerfully; all money should be sent forth fearlessly and with a blessing.'

Current law of attraction experts, such as those in the film *The Secret* and writers including Gabrielle Bernstein and Kyle Gray, talk about this 'attitude of gratitude' when paying for anything. This means taking a moment to appreciate that you have the finances to pay the bill, feeling grateful for where that money has come from and that you have enough. Sign cheques and pay bills by writing 'Paid with love and thanks' on the back of them. Even though many bills are paid online nowadays, you can still write down a list of your bills or debts to be paid, and as you pay and tick each one off, write your thanks in the margin, feeling the full appreciation that you are able to pay all you need to, even if it is small amounts toward the final balance. See yourself paying off the final amount and being debt-free. As Shinn says, 'The vision and action must go hand-in-hand, as in the case of the man who bought the fur-lined overcoat.'

Acting *as if*

Remember, it is not necessary to get yourself into financial difficulty by performing overly extravagant acts of faith; many actions cost nothing. Simply window-shopping for whatever you want, connecting with it often in your mind every time you notice it, creates an invisible connection with that thing. Sooner or later it will be drawn into your life. Create new daily behaviours to upshift your beliefs about yourself and what you can achieve, and all you desire will manifest. Mike Dooley, in his book *Infinite Possibilities*, suggests the following ideas for *acting as if* you already have what your heart truly wants.

For full, radiant health:

- If you are ill in bed and longing to get outside for a walk, a way to act *as if* you were already walking might be to check the weather every day and imagine yourself getting out in it. Visualize how wonderful it will be to feel the sun on your face, or feel the crunch of autumn leaves under your feet, as you swing your arms and move your body along a path in nature.

- When or if able to move, but confined to your home, you could still take a walk around your house, or do some light stretching to prepare your body for more strenuous exertion.

- To improve your health overall, spend a day or two eating only what a super-healthy person would eat. Then, see if you could incorporate aspects of that diet every day, feeling good about yourself whatever small steps you take to vibrant wellness.

- Reminder – all activities need to be supported by eating well and checking with your doctor first.

Becoming a magnet for romance:

- Set the place at your dinner table or create space in your closet for your lover when they move in.

- Buy or make little gifts as if they are for a new partner, such as picking a bunch of flowers from your garden or choosing a tie from a charity shop.

- Book a second ticket to something you'd like to take a significant other to. It doesn't have to be an expensive event; there are many free gigs or activities you could act as if you are taking a boyfriend or girlfriend to.

Attracting a new or better job:
- As well as doing all the usual job-hunting activities, including updating your CV, looking through employment adverts and applying for positions, you can also start acting as if your dream career is here.

- Get up at the time you would to go to work a few mornings a week, put on your work clothes and leave the house, even if just for a walk.

- If you haven't got the right clothes for the job you want, you could borrow from friends or try on a few items in shops and feel how it would be to wear them every day for work.

- You could visit prospective employers' offices or sites to have a look and imagine yourself there.

- Go for a coffee or have lunch with a friend in the area where future colleagues hang out, imagining you're on your work break.

- If you want to start your own business, write down your company mission statement or what you want to achieve. Brainstorm a brand name, sketch your logo, play around with building your website on free sites such as Weebly or Wix.

- Plan and window-shop for the gift you'll give yourself when you double your sales or reach another business goal.

Acting as if money is abundant:

- Similar to tithing, a great way to build the belief that you have plenty of money is to give to charity. It doesn't have to be much, but any little helps others. Feel grateful that you are in a position to donate to those that need it more, trusting that your funds will be replenished by the universal flow of energy.

- If you can, increase your minimum payments on any debts by a small amount every week. As long as it's affordable, this action can help bust the blocks to abundance by knowing you are paying down anything you owe even more quickly.

Prosperity is incoming:

- Test drive some fancy cars at a dealership if a new automobile is what you're after, or ring up anyone selling your dream car and ask for more details.

- If long-distance travel is your desire, get your passport ready, look through brochures and plan the perfect trip – the more out-of-the-ordinary the better.

- Plan a celebration party for that book published or exam passed. Look around possible venues and imagine your crowd of partygoers there. Write the guest list and invitations, arrange the music playlist or research bands to play.

Try to do all of the above with a sense of fun. The more playful and enjoyable the *acting as if* can be, the more you are likely to do it often, to change your beliefs and raise your frequency in alignment with what is rightfully yours. Keep on acting in the faith that all you dream of will indeed manifest, as long as you don't block it with opposing, fearful or anxious thoughts or actions. Often, doing something really brave that takes you completely out of your comfort zone demonstrates huge faith and acts even more in your favour. Shinn shares this example of how facing our fears with one bold move can completely change our circumstances:

'There was a man who had lost all his money. He was living in very poor quarters, all the people around him were poor and he was afraid to spend the little he had. All he had was about five dollars. He had tried to work but everyone had turned him down. He awoke one morning to face another day of lack and disappointment, when the idea (or hunch) came to him to go to the horse show. It took about all he had but he was fired with the idea of being with rich and successful people again. He was tired of his limited surroundings. He fearlessly spent the money for a ticket to the horse show. There he met an old friend, who said, "Hello Jim! Where have you been all this time?" Before the show was over the old friend gave him a wonderful position in his firm. His hunch and

fearless attitude toward money had put him in a new vibration of success.'

Taking a giant leap of faith and doing something different can really raise your frequency to the level of success and put you in alignment with better circumstances. As Shinn says, 'Form the habit of making giant swings into faith. You will receive marvellous returns.' It's how the law of attraction works, when you align your thoughts, words, faith and actions to receive all that your heart desires.

Be passionate about what you do, but keep plans to yourself

One vital element that helps this alignment is to truly be yourself, and be genuinely interested in everything you do, from your creative self-expression and hobbies to your employment. As Shinn says, 'Taking an interest in your work, enjoying what you are doing, opens the secret door to success…If you want to be interesting to others, be interested in something. An interested person is an enthusiastic person…Many people are without vital interests and are hungry to hear what other people are doing…They must be entertained every minute. Their own affairs do not hold enough interest…It is dangerous to neglect your own affairs and to take an idle curiosity in what others are doing. We should all be busily engaged in perfecting ourselves, but take a kindly interest in others.'

When you are true to yourself and on a path of self-development, following your *own* interests and career path, she says, 'Then you can expand rapidly into the Divine plan of your life where you fulfil your destiny. You may be sure that the Divine plan of your life will give you perfect satisfaction. You will no

After all, we are all individuals here to express our God-essence through our experiences. As even Plato said, centuries ago: 'There is a place that you are here to fill and no one else can fill, something you are to do, which no one else can do.'

Once you have discovered what this is, through deep introspection and self-awareness, try to keep your plans to yourself. When you reveal all the details of your dream with someone, you risk them ridiculing, belittling or judging it, doing it themselves or gossiping about it to others. This can diminish your goal and reduce your confidence to carry it out. So, Shinn says, 'Talk about your affairs as little as possible, and then only to the ones who will give you encouragement and inspiration. The world is full of "wet blankets", people who tell you "It can't be done," that you're aiming too high.'

But don't give up. Persevere with courage and determination to succeed. 'The road to success is a straight and narrow path; it is a road of loving absorption, of undivided attention,' says Shinn.

Mulford agrees: 'Persistent resolve on any purpose is a real attractive force or element, drawing constantly more and more aids for carrying out that resolve... all your discreet talk, your interest and persistent determination, represent for you so much actual outlay of force expended in attracting the thing desired to you.'

of force expended in attracting the thing desired to you.'

So, act on your intentions, step-by-step; prepare for your blessings as if they are already here; and stay focused on the end result. Let no one come between you and your dreams, and allow the energy to build to bring all you want into your life.

CHAPTER 5

HOLDING A CLEAR VISION

A major part of attracting everything you want is seeing it happen and holding that vision in your mind as you undertake all the actions it takes to get there. To be rich, or happy, or fully healthy you must see yourself as such, having faith that your visions will come true. When you can see yourself living a prosperous, successful life, full of wonderful experiences and incredible relationships, you are more likely to believe it can happen. Then, through your actions in alignment with your visions, all you desire will manifest.

As Shinn writes, with her usual referencing of Bible passages, 'Man can only receive what he sees himself receiving. The children of Israel were told that they could have all the land they could see. This is true of every man. He has only the land within his own mental vision. Every great work, every big accomplishment has been brought into manifestation through holding to the vision, and often just before the big achievement, comes apparent failure and discouragement. However, the one who knows spiritual law, is undisturbed by appearance... he holds to his vision and gives thanks that the end is accomplished, he has received... It may be perfect health, love, supply, self-expression, home or friends. They are all finished and perfect ideas registered in Divine Mind (man's own superconscious mind) and must come through him, not to him.'

Another law of attraction writer, Wallace D Wattles, in his book *The Science of Getting Rich* (1910), agrees: 'Man must form a clear and definite mental image of the things he wishes to have, to do, or to become; and he must hold this mental image in his thoughts, while being deeply grateful to the Supreme that all his desires are granted to him.'

He also explains that you do not need to visualize every step along the way – you simply have to follow your creative urges and inspirations to get to the end goal: 'It is not your part to guide or supervise the creative process; all you have to do with that is to retain your vision, stick to your purpose, and maintain your faith and gratitude.'

So if you want to change your career path or find a new job, Wattles says, 'Hold the vision of yourself in the right business, with the purpose to get into it, and the faith that you will get into it, and are getting into it; but act in your present business. Use your present business as the means of getting a better one, and use your present environment as the means of getting a better one. Your vision of the right business, if held with faith and purpose, will cause the Supreme to move the right business toward you; and your action...will cause you to move toward the business... Hold the vision of yourself in the job you want, while you act with faith and purpose on the job you have, and you will certainly get the job you want...Your vision and faith will set the creative force in motion to bring it toward you, and your action will cause the forces in your own environment to move you toward the place you want.'

Help this process along by stating another of Shinn's affirmations:

'Let me now express the Divine Idea in my mind, body and affairs.'

She adds, 'If you will impress the subconscious by repeating this statement you will be amazed at the changes which soon take place. You will be bombarded by new ideas and new ideals. A chemical change will take place in your body. Your environment will change for the better, for you are expanding rapidly into the Divine Plan, where all conditions are permanently perfect.'

All you desire is already manifest

In the quantum field, or superconscious mind, all you desire is already available for you as soon as you ask for it. Shinn explains more: 'In the superconscious (or Christ within) there is a lavish supply for every demand, and your good is perfect and permanent... [but] with the average person (who has thought in terms of lack for a long time) it is very difficult to build up a rich consciousness...You must have a great desire for financial freedom, you must feel yourself rich, you must see yourself rich, you must continually prepare for riches. Become as a little child and make believe you are rich. You are then impressing the subconscious with expectancy.'

The more you tune into the stillness within, connect with God/Source/Infinite Intelligence, the more visions will come to you about what is waiting for you on your path. Then, to help you really see and feel all you are here to explore and experience, use your imagination and play-act as if all that you desire is already happening.

All the ideas and suggestions in the previous chapter for *acting as if* can be used to prepare you for the many blessings coming to you. Small, regular tasks and changes in behaviour build the pictures of preparedness for your dream foreign holiday, new fast car or top job. Utilize this creative faculty of your mind daily to dream your ideal life into being.

Shinn clarifies using the Bible quote: 'Out of the imaginations of the heart come the issues of life.' It is by tuning into what your heart truly wants, and imagining those desires with the creative part of the mind, that we get into the flow of our destiny, or divine plan, and attract all that is rightfully ours.

'When people have lost the power to imagine their good, they "perish" (or go under),' explains Shinn, quoting the Bible. 'Without the vision (imagination) my people perish, in lack and limitation. You may work very hard on the external and accomplish nothing, if you are without vision. Vision means to see clearly where you are going. To keep your eye on the goal. All men who have accomplished big things have done this...Clear vision is like a man with a compass; he knows where he is going...You can never do a thing you cannot see yourself doing, or fill a place

you cannot see yourself
filling – not visualizing,
making a mental picture
(this is a mental process
and often brings wrong
and limited results);
it must be a spiritual
realization, a feeling that
you are already there; be
in its vibration.'

To illustrate this point
of feeling the vibration
of success, Shinn tells
the story of a famous
footballer, 'the greatest
all-round athlete in
the world, who trained
lying in a hammock.' His
trainer wanted him to
get up and do something
but instead he just
closed his eyes and saw
himself doing his sport
successfully – all from
his relaxed position in
his hammock. Many
champion sportspeople

today practise similar creative visualization. They imagine themselves scoring the winning goal, crossing the finish line, taking first place on the winner's podium, and it invariably happens exactly as they see it in their mind's eye – because all through their training they held that vision of their goal in their mind, body and spirit, and felt it happen with all their being.

Wattles explains this practice further: 'You must hold your vision while you are doing each act, however trivial or commonplace…It should be the work of your leisure hours to use your imagination on the details of your vision, and to contemplate them until they are firmly fixed upon your memory. If you wish speedy results, spend practically all your spare time in this practice. By continuous contemplation you will get the picture of what you want, even to the smallest details, so firmly fixed upon your mind… that in your working hours you need only to mentally refer to the picture to stimulate your faith and purpose, and cause your best effort to be put forth. Contemplate your picture in your leisure hours until your consciousness is so full of it that you can grasp it instantly. You will become so enthused with its bright promises that the mere thought of it will call forth the strongest energies of your whole being.'

Developing the imagination and daydreaming

about what you want generally speeds up the
manifestation process, as you are attracting your
desires from a relaxed state of natural creativity.
Wattles says, 'A day or two spent...contemplating the
vision of what you want, and in earnest thanksgiving
that you are getting it, will bring your mind into such
close relationships with the Supreme that you will
make no mistake when you do act.'

Positive thoughts, positive visions

If whatever you see in your imagination is likely to
happen in your life, Shinn asks us to delve deeper
into what we are visualizing: 'What are you seeing
with your inner eye? What pictures are you inviting
into your life?' Make sure they are not negated by

habitual thoughts of failure. A powerful, descriptive affirmation can help you come up with the right images. Shinn gave the following phrase to another of her clients to help conjure up the imagery of riches with a magic purse: 'As money goes out, immediately money comes in, under grace in perfect ways. I see it always crammed, jammed with money: yellow bills, green bills, pink cheques, blue cheques, white cheques, gold, silver and currency. I see it bulging with abundance!

'The affirmation of the magic purse is very powerful,' says Shinn, 'as it brings a vivid picture to mind. It is impossible not to see your purse or wallet filled with money when using the words "crammed, jammed". Choose words which bring a flash of the fulfilment of the demand. Never force a picture by visualizing it; let the Divine Idea flash into your conscious mind; then the student is working according to the Divine Design.'

Shinn explains the difference between visualizing and visioning. 'Visualizing is a mental process governed by the reasoning or conscious mind; visioning is a spiritual process, governed by intuition or the superconscious mind. The student should train his mind to receive these flashes of inspiration, and work out the "divine pictures" through definite leads. When a man can say, "*I desire only that which God desires for me*," his false desires fade from the consciousness, and a new set of blueprints is given to him by the Master Architect, the God within. God's plan for each man transcends the limitation of the reasoning mind...many a man is building for himself in imagination a bungalow when he should be building a palace.'

So, while it's good to spend time imagining the things you want in great and glorious detail, you have to allow divinity to bring you those visions in the first place – for it may have even better things in mind. Spend time connecting to Source to receive flashes of inspiration and visions of what your divine plan has in store for you, then start to imagine the end result, feeling how it will be when all you desire manifests. You could make a vision board to help with this, as a relaxing and creative way to enhance your visions of all you wish for.

The key to the law of attraction working for you is not forcing your will to attain certain goals that

How to make a vision board

Find a large piece of paper and glue a photo of yourself in the centre.

- Look through magazines for images or print off pictures online of all the things you would love to have in your life. It could be photos of your dream home, the furniture in it, the new, fast car parked on the drive and the beautiful flower-filled garden. It might be images of friends having fun together or a romantic sunset walk on the beach with a lover. It might be a business mentor you'd like to meet, to get help with a career project.

- Cut out and collect any pictures that spur the imagination to dream about your perfect life. Now glue these images on the piece of paper in a way that is pleasing to you around your portrait image.

- As you do this task, allow your imagination to run wild, visualizing all the wonderful objects, experiences and people you'd love to have in your life. Really feel the feelings of fulfilment, love, happiness and success connected to all these aspects of your dream life.

- Stick this vision board where you can see it

daily, to help nudge your imagination again whenever you see it.

- Don't get hung up on the details of how to attract all these things into your life. Trust that the universal flow of energy/divinity/God will guide you towards them through flashes of divine inspiration leading you on to the next step on your path to fulfilling your heart's desires.

suggest success, wealth or happiness, but trusting in God's plan for you to manifest in all its glory. Allow the divine design of your life to unfold through you, by listening to your intuition and receiving visions directly from Source to guide you along your path to fulfilment. Tune into the divine design of your life, your body and affairs, and imagine it at its highest, most perfect level.

When you want to draw more money from a bank to finance a new business, treat your family, or buy something you've always dreamed of, first harness the powers of another bank. As Shinn says, 'We all have a bank we can draw upon, the Bank of the Imagination. Let us imagine ourselves rich, well and happy: imagine all our affairs in divine order; but leave the way of fulfilment to Infinite Intelligence.'

CHAPTER 6

TIMING

Perhaps the hardest part of manifesting all you desire is having the patience to wait for 'right timing'. Instead of desperately wanting everything to happen straight away, you have to remain patient and trust, with calm certainty, that your goals and visions will come about whenever they are designed to, according to your divine plan. Many things just take longer to manifest. Remember, a large, beautiful oak tree is there in the acorn, but it takes time to grow into its magnificence.

Contrary to what contemporary society tells us, faster isn't always better. As spiritual teacher, healer and life coach Christina Lopes says, 'The belief that "faster is better" has created one major fallacy...that the best way from point A to point B is a straight line...But sometimes the best path to your desires and dreams is through detours and changes of course. Sometimes the goals you had in your mind weren't in harmony with what your soul truly wants, so life puts a wall in front of you to show you another way. Sometimes life puts walls in front of you to soften you, to teach you to flow, to be flexible, to trust and have patience...Sometimes life needs to mature in order to bring you amazing gifts and delights. Sometimes you need to mature and transform in order to receive what you're asking for.'

Lopes suggests 'thinking like a farmer' when you're feeling impatience at things not working out as quickly as you'd like. 'Farmers are masters at knowing that everything has a season and needs time to mature. A farmer plants a seed, waters it and patiently waits for it to turn into a crop. Learn to cultivate the art of allowing life to be slow when it needs to be, always understanding that divine timing is the best timing for you. Remember that life is working for you. See pauses as guidance and love from the universe, not punishment. When life seems to close all doors you may be going through a spiritual awakening stage called The Void, a time of pause, cocooning and internal metamorphosis. So slow down and flow more with life.'

However, when there is a delay in something you want coming into your life, fears and doubts are more likely to arise, pushing all you dream of further away with their negative energy. If you're not extra

conscious and careful with your thoughts at this time, you might attract troublesome situations to reflect your worries and beliefs that 'things don't work out for you.'

As Shinn says, 'The average person will dwell on all the obstacles and hindrances which are there to prevent his good coming to pass. You combine with what you notice so if you give obstacles and hindrances your undivided attention, they grow worse... Do not magnify obstacles, magnify...God's power.'

Magic-magnifying meditation

To clear your mind and fully connect with the Christ light within you, which is unfolding through you in everything that comes up in your life, try a visualization as you sit in meditation. Shinn says, 'See yourself, daily, bathed in the Light of the Christ. This inner radiance is invincible power and dissolves anything not Divinely planned. It dissolves all appearance of disease, lack, loss or limitation. It dissolves adverse conditions, or "any weapon that is formed against you".

Imagine a bright white light filling your whole body and expanding out into your aura

and your environment, as far as you wish, purifying everything it comes into contact with and raising your frequency to its highest level. See this white auric field around you cleared of any energy that isn't yours and radiating all your bright Christ energy out into the world. You could imagine an indigo magnetic field around this white aura which repels anything not meant for you and attracts all that is designed for you. Sit in this meditation as long as it feels good. Then go about your day with the awareness that you are Source energy in a human form, attracting only that which resonates at the same frequency.

Affirm your faith in positive outcomes

Keep repeating affirmations that reassure your faith in the power of divinity helping everything work out for you at exactly the right time (see Chapter 2: Power of Words). As Shinn says, 'Spirit is never too late…We hear people saying: "My good always comes to me too late." "I've lost so many opportunities!" We must reverse the thought and say repeatedly:

> ## "I am awake to my good. I never miss a trick."
>
> Or
>
> ## "Nothing can hinder, nothing can delay the manifesting of the Divine Plan of my life."

Remember, a situation can often appear to get worse before it gets better. It's the 'darkness before the dawn' phenomenon that Shinn writes a lot about, including this example of, 'a man who was so poor and discouraged, that he ended it all. A few days later, came a letter notifying him that he had inherited a large fortune...do not be fooled by the darkness before the dawn...When one has made his demands upon the Universal, he must be ready for surprises. Everything may seem to be going wrong, when in reality, it is going right.'

As Wallace Wattles explains, when things go wrong, it's likely that what you thought was right for you is not, and that something better is coming instead. 'Never allow yourself to feel disappointed,' he says. 'You may expect to have a certain thing at a certain time, and not get it at that time; and this will appear to you like failure. But if you hold to your faith you will find that the failure is only apparent…if you do not receive that thing, you will receive something so much better that you will see the seeming failure was really a great success.'

He shares the story of someone who had set his mind on 'a certain business combination, which seemed to him at the time to be very desirable, and he worked for some weeks to bring it about. When the crucial time came, the thing failed in a perfectly inexplicable way; it was as if some unseen influence had been working secretly against him. He was not disappointed; on the contrary, he thanked God that his desire had been overruled, and went steadily on with his grateful mind. In a few weeks, an opportunity so much better came his way that he would not have made the first deal on any account; and he saw that a Mind which knew more than he knew had prevented him from losing the greater good by entangling himself with the lesser.'

Shinn agrees: 'You may think all your happiness depends upon obtaining one particular thing in life; later on, you praise the Lord that you didn't get it.'

Cultivate gratitude

While waiting for whatever you want to come into
your life, don't do it from a state of lack. Hold a
feeling of appreciation for all the blessings already in
your life and those incoming. Cultivating a continual
attitude of gratitude elevates the mind to the level of
loving awareness of all the good that surrounds you,
helping to manifest more of it.

As Wattles says, you actually come into alignment
with Source energy, 'by entertaining a lively and
sincere gratitude for the blessings it bestows...
Gratitude unifies the mind of man with the
intelligence...Man can remain upon the creative plane
only by uniting himself with the Formless Intelligence
through a deep and continuous feeling of gratitude.'

List 10 things you are grateful for *right now*, and 10 more things that you are thankful for throughout your life. Even seemingly 'bad' things can provoke a feeling of gratitude, as they may have led to something better. Write a letter of thanks for the things you want to happen as if you'd just received them.

Come back to the present moment

To help you relax while you wait for your dreams to actualize, regularly tune into the peace inside of you. Sitting in stillness calms any anxiety and connects you to the universal energy, where all is well, right here, right now, in this present moment – and from where everything manifests. Lorie Ladd talks about how to connect to stillness and how important it is:

'Drop into what is. Breathe. Settle into what is, even if it's not what you want or feels bad. It is what it is. Be present. From that point of settled stillness the next steps forward arise, in a calm way. Being in a state of calm in the midst of a storm is the way through the storm, not letting thoughts run away with us into anxiety, fearing the thing we want won't happen. Relax. Stop using excess energy to fight against what is. Go with the flow, as much as you don't want to. You will get into a place of ease, of peace, even when things don't feel good.'

Ladd insists that feeling all of our feelings, even the ones we don't like, helps them flow through us and takes us to new states of awareness. Here we can cope with everything – including waiting for what we want to happen – but from a state of presence rather than clinging to past actions or emotions, or fretting over the future.

Shinn writes, 'Remember, now is the appointed time! Today is the day! And your good can happen overnight.' However, 'Living in the past is a failure method and a violation of spiritual law. Jesus Christ said, "Behold, now is the accepted time," and "Now is the day of Salvation." The robbers of time are the past and future. Man should bless the past, and forget it, if it keeps him in bondage, and bless the future, knowing it has in store endless joys, but live *fully in the now*. Man must live suspended in the moment. He must be spiritually alert, ever waiting [for] his leads, taking advantage of every opportunity.'

Tune into your own guidance, not that from others

While it might be tempting to turn to the tarot cards or astrology to help predict exactly when your dreams will come true, it's better to focus on following your own internal compass. Says Shinn, 'I have found it destructive to look to the psychic plane for guidance, as it is the plane of many minds and not

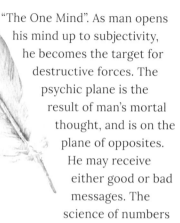

"The One Mind". As man opens his mind up to subjectivity, he becomes the target for destructive forces. The psychic plane is the result of man's mortal thought, and is on the plane of opposites. He may receive either good or bad messages. The science of numbers [numerology] and the reading of horoscopes keep man down on the mental (or mortal) plane, for they deal only with the Karmic path...However, if any good message has ever been given one, of coming happiness, or wealth, harbour and expect it, and it will manifest sooner or later, through the law of expectancy. Man's will should be used to back the universal will. *I will that the will of God be done.* It is God's will to give every man every righteous desire of his heart, and man's will should be used to hold the perfect vision, without wavering.'

Cultivate joyful expectancy, like a child waiting for their presents on Christmas morning. Shinn says to think of, 'the little boy who asked for a drum for Christmas. The child does not lie awake at night

agonizing over his drum wondering whether he will get it. He goes to bed and sleeps like a top. He jumps out of bed in the morning ready for the happy day before him. He looks with wonder at that which is before him.

'Children are filled with happy expectancy until grown-up people and unhappy experiences bring them out of the world of the wondrous,' Shinn states, repeating phrases such as, 'Don't expect too much, then you will be disappointed,' 'You can't have everything in this life,' 'Childhood is your happiest time,' and 'No one knows what the future will bring.'

Such gloomy mantras harm a child's sense of wonder and excitement that diminishes them through adulthood. Today, children are made to worry about the state of the planet, wars and deadly viruses, stopping their natural joy and hope at what's to come. Such daily depressive news stories and grown-up worries quash a child's enthusiasm for life and the future, forming beliefs that get in the way of the wondrous where true happiness and success are found.

It takes strength of mind and spirit to retain a sense of miracle consciousness, especially through troubling times that seem to go on forever without changing. But transformation will come if you stay dedicated to your path, through positive affirmations, inspiring vision and faith in divine timing to manifest all your dreams.

CHAPTER 7

Final Words

Ultimately, living according to the law of attraction is about connecting more to our internal light and allowing that great, expansive consciousness within us to express itself more and more through us. Connecting to and working with this ever-expanding divinity, through our thoughts, words, visions and actions, means manifesting all that's in alignment with this power. As Mulford wrote over a century ago, 'As we learn to draw this infinite wisdom to us, it means ever-perfecting health, greater and greater power to enjoy all that exists, gradual transition into a higher state of being and the development of powers ... We are the limited yet ever-growing parts and expressions of the Supreme Never-Ending Whole.'

The more of us that align with this Christ consciousness within, and create the lives we want from there, the more others will also be able to do the

same. 'It is a wise selfishness that works to benefit others along with ourselves,' says Mulford. 'Because in spirit, and in actual element, we are all united. We are forces which act and react on each other, for good or ill, through what ignorantly we call "empty space." There are unseen nerves extending from man to man, from being to being. Every form of life is in this sense connected together. We are all "members of one body."'

Mulford, like all law of attraction experts, is stating the deep truth of existence: that we are all one consciousness, always expanding and expressing itself through all of life. Everything is connected, because it is all part of the same infinite intelligence. So whatever you are doing to bring more of your dynamic truth to light, to express your creativity, to enhance your health, wealth and wellbeing, serves the greater good and enables more people to shine their light just as brilliantly.

All law of attraction experts believe that this universal energy is love in action. Not a romantic kind of love, but the love of God, in manifestation. It's the strongest magnetic force in the universe and can help us create the most incredible lives imaginable. Shinn agrees: 'We should all build up in our consciousness a picture of peace, harmony and beauty, and someday it will push itself into visibility.' We don't need to doubt ourselves, she says, for 'We are fully equipped for the Divine Plan of our lives. We are more than equal to every situation.'

Knowing and living this realization will open us up to the love of divinity as it moves us into our path of joy, abundance and peace. If we could simply align with this realization, says Shinn, 'We could actually hear the hum of Divine activity, for we would be linked with Infinite Intelligence which knows no defeat. Opportunities would come to us from unexpected quarters. Divine activity would operate in and through all our affairs and the Divine Idea would come to pass.'

So let's align with this wondrous, ever-expanding love at the heart of all creation to manifest the brightest, best and highest potential for humanity and the whole world.

Florence's Own Words

This book has drawn on the works of New Thought writers. Among the best of these writers was Florence Scovel Shinn (1871-1940). Here we present extracts from her addresses to audiences on the subject of attracting success and manifesting your greatest good. They must be read in the context with references to phrases, celebrities, items, and daily life, contemporary to her time.

Look With Wonder

I will remember the works of the Lord; surely I will remember thy wonders of old.

Psalms 77:11

The words wonder and wonderful are used many times in the Bible. In the dictionary the word wonder is defined as, "a cause for surprise, astonishment, a miracle, a marvel."

Ouspensky, in his book, *Tertium Organum*, calls the 4th dimensional world, the "World of the Wondrous." He has figured out mathematically, that there is a realm where all conditions are perfect. Jesus Christ called it the Kingdom.

We might say, "Seek ye first the world of the wondrous, and all things shall be added unto you."

It can only be reached through a state of consciousness.

Jesus Christ said, to enter the Kingdom we must become "as a little child." Children are continually in a state of joy and wonder!

The future holds promises of mysterious good. Anything can happen overnight.

Robert Louis Stevenson, in *A Child's Garden of Verses* says: "The world is so full of a number of things. I'm sure we should all be as happy as kings."

So let us look with wonder at that which is before us; that statement was given me a number of years ago, I mention it in my book, *The Game of Life and How To Play It*.

I had missed an opportunity and felt that I should have been more awake to my good. The next day, I took the statement early in the morning, "I look with wonder at that which is before me."

At noon the phone rang, and the proposition was put to me again. This time I grasped it. I did indeed, look with wonder for I never expected the opportunity to come to me again.

A friend in one of my meetings said the other day, that this statement had brought her wonderful results. It fills the consciousness with happy expectancy.

Children are filled with happy expectancy until grown-up people, and unhappy experiences, bring them out of the world of the wondrous!

Let us look back and remember some of the gloomy ideas which were given us: "Eat the speckled apples first." "Don't expect too much, then you won't be disappointed." "You can't have everything in this life." "Childhood is your happiest time." "No one knows what the future will bring." What a start in life!

These are some of the impressions I picked up in early childhood. At the age of six I had a great sense

of responsibility. Instead of looking with wonder at that which was before me, I looked with fear and suspicion. I feel much younger now than I did when I was six.

I have an early photograph taken about that time, grasping a flower, but with a careworn and hopeless expression. I had left the world of the wondrous behind me! I was now living in the world of realities, as my elders told me and it was far from wondrous.

It is a great privilege for children to live in this age, when they are taught Truth from their birth. Even if they are not taught actual metaphysics, the ethers are filled with joyous expectancy.

You may become a Shirley Temple or a Freddy Bartholomew or a great pianist at the age of six and go on a concert tour.

We are all now back in the world of the wondrous, where anything can happen overnight, for when miracles do come, they come quickly! So let us become Miracle Conscious and prepare for miracles, expect miracles, and we are then inviting them into our lives.

Maybe you need a financial miracle! There is a supply for every demand. Through active faith, the word and intuition, we release this invisible supply.

I will give an example: One of my students found herself almost without funds, she needed one thousand dollars, and she had had plenty of money at one time and beautiful possessions, but had nothing left but an ermine wrap. No fur dealer would give her much for it.

I spoke the word that it would be sold to the right person for the right price, or that the supply would come in some other way. It was necessary that the money manifest at once, it was no time to worry or reason.

She was on the street making her affirmations. It was a stormy day. She said to herself, "I'm going to show active faith in my invisible supply by taking a taxi cab." It was a very strong hunch. As she got out of the taxi, at her destination, a woman stood waiting to get in.

It was an old friend, a very, very kind friend. It was the first time in her life she had ever taken a taxi, but her Rolls Royce was out of commission that afternoon.

They talked and my friend told her about the ermine wrap. "Why," her friend said, "I will give you a thousand dollars for it." And that afternoon she had the cheque.

God's ways are ingenious, His methods are sure.

A student wrote me the other day, that she was using that statement: "God's ways are ingenious, His methods are sure." A series of unexpected contacts brought about a situation she had been desiring. She looked with wonder at the working of the law.

Our demonstrations usually come within a "split second." All is timed with amazing accuracy in Divine Mind.

My student left the taxi, just as her friend stopped to enter; a second later, she would have hailed another taxi.

Man's part is to be wide awake to his leads and hunches; for on the magic path of Intuition is all that he desires or requires.

In Moulton's Modern Reader's Bible, the book of Psalms is recognized as the perfection of lyric poetry.

"The musical meditation which

is the essence of lyrics can find no higher field than the devout spirit which at once raises itself to the service of God, and overflows on the various sides of active and contemplative life."

The Psalms are also human documents, and I have selected the 77th Psalm because it gives the picture of a man in despair, but as he contemplates the wonders of God, faith and assurance are restored to him.

I cried unto God with my voice, even unto God with my voice; and He gave ear unto me.

In the day of my trouble I sought the Lord, my soul refused to be comforted.

Will the Lord cast off forever? And will he be favourable no more?

Hath God forgotten to be gracious? Hath he in anger shut up his tender mercies?

And I said, This is my infirmity, but I will remember the years of the right hand of the Most High.

I will meditate also of all thy work, and talk of thy doings.

Thy way, O God, is in the sanctuary, who is so great a God as our God!

Thou art the God that doest wonders.

Thou hast with thine arm redeemed thy people.

This is a picture of what the average Truth student goes through when confronted with a problem. He is assailed by thoughts of doubt, fear and despair.

Then some statement of Truth will flash into his consciousness—"God's ways are ingenious, His methods are sure!" He remembers other difficulties which have been overcome, his confidence in God returns. He thinks, "what God has done before, He will do for me and more!"

I was talking to a friend not long ago who said, "I would be pretty dumb if I didn't believe God could solve my problem. So many times before, wonderful things have come to me, I know they will come again!"

So the summing up of the 77th Psalm is, "What God has done before, he now does for me and more!"

It is a good thing to say when you think of your past success, happiness or wealth. All loss comes from your own vain imaginings, fear of loss crept into your consciousness, you carried burdens and fought battles, you reasoned instead of sticking to the magic path of intuition.

But in the twinkling of an eye, all will be restored to you, for as they say in the East, "What Allah has given, cannot be diminished."

Now to go back to the child's state of consciousness, you should be filled with wonder, but be careful not to live in your past childhood.

I know people who can only think about their happy childhood days. They remember what they wore! No skies have since been so blue, or grass so green. They therefore miss the opportunities of the wonderful now.

I will tell an amusing story of a friend who lived in a town when she was very young, then moved away to another city. She always looked back to the house they first lived in, to her it was an enchanted palace, large, spacious and glamorous.

Many years after, when she had grown up, she had an opportunity of visiting this house. She was disillusioned, she found it small, stuffy and ugly. Her idea of beauty had entirely changed, for in the front yard was an iron dog.

If you went back to your past, it would not be the same. So in this friend's family, they called living in the past, "iron dogging."

Her sister told me a story of some "iron dogging" she had done. When she was about sixteen, she met abroad, a very dashing and romantic young man, an artist. This romance didn't last long, but she talked about it a lot to the man she afterwards married.

Years rolled by, the dashing and romantic young man, had become a well-known artist and came to this country to have an exhibition of his pictures. My friend was filled with excitement, and hunted him up to renew their friendship. She went to his exhibition, and in walked a portly business man, no trace was left of the dashing romantic youth! When she told her husband, all he said was, "iron dogging."

Remember, now is the appointed time! Today is the day! And your good can happen overnight.

Look with wonder at that which is before you! We are filled with divine expectancy, "I will restore to you the years which the locusts have eaten!"

Now let each one think of the good which seems so difficult to attain. It may be health, wealth, happiness or perfect self-expression.

Do not think how your good can be accomplished, just give thanks that you have already received on the invisible plane, "therefore the steps leading up to it are secured also." Be wide awake to your intuitive leads, and suddenly, you find yourself in your Promised Land.

"I look with wonder at that which is before me."

Catch Up With Your Good

And it shall come to pass, that before they call,
I will answer; and while they are yet speaking,
I will hear.

Isaiah 65:24

Catch up with your good! This is a new way of saying, "Before they call, I will answer." Your good precedes you; it gets there before you do. But how to catch up with your good? For you must have ears that hear, and eyes that see, or it will escape you.

Some people never catch up with their good in life; they will say, "My life has always been one of hardship, no good luck ever comes to me." They are the people who have been asleep to their opportunities; or through laziness, haven't caught up with their good.

A woman told a group of friends that she had not eaten for three days. They dashed about asking people to give her work; but she refused it. She explained that she never got up until twelve o'clock, she liked to lie in bed and read magazines.

She just wanted people to support her while she read *Vogue* and *Harper's Bazaar*. We must be careful not to slip into lazy states of mind.

Take the affirmation, "I am wide awake to my good, I never miss a trick." Most people are only half awake to their good.

A student said to me, "If I don't follow my hunches, I always get into a jam."

I will tell the story of a woman, one of my students, who followed her intuitive leads which brought amazing results.

She had been asked to visit friends in a nearby town. She had very little money. When she arrived at her destination, she found the house locked up. They had gone away. She was filled with despair, then commenced to pray. She said, "Infinite Intelligence, give me a definite lead, let me know just what to do!"

The name of a certain hotel flashed into her consciousness, it persisted, the name seemed to stand out in big letters.

She had just enough money to get back to New York and the hotel. As she was about to enter, an old friend suddenly appeared, who greeted her warmly and whom she hadn't seen in years.

She explained that she was living at the hotel but was going away for several months, and added, "Why don't you live in my suite while I am away, it won't cost you a cent." My friend accepted gratefully, and looked with amazement on the working of Spiritual Law. She had caught up with her good by following intuition.

All going forward comes from desire. Science today, is going back to Lamarck and his "wishing theory." He claims that birds do not fly because they have wings, but they have wings because they wanted to fly; the result of the "push of the emotional wish."

Think of the irresistible power of thought with clear vision. Many people are in a fog most of the time, making wrong decisions and going the wrong way.

During the Christmas rush, my maid said to a saleswoman at one of the big shops, "I suppose this is your busiest day." She replied, "Oh no! The day after Christmas is our busiest day, when people bring most of the things back."

Hundreds of people choosing the wrong gifts because they were not listening to their intuitive leads.

No matter what you are doing, ask for guidance. It saves time and energy and often a lifetime of misery.

All suffering comes from the violation of intuition. Unless intuition builds the house, they labor in vain who build it.

Get the habit of hunching, then you will always be on the magic path.

"And it shall come to pass, that before they call, I will answer, and while they are yet speaking, I will hear."

Working with spiritual law, we are bringing to pass that which already is. In the Universal Mind it is there as an idea, but is crystallized on the external, by a sincere desire.

The idea of a bird was a perfect picture in divine mind, the fish caught the idea, and wished themselves into birds.

Are your desires bringing you wings? We should all be bringing some seemingly impossible thing to pass.

One of my affirmations is, "The unexpected happens, my seemingly impossible good now comes to pass."

Do not magnify obstacles, magnify the Lord—that means, magnify God's power.

The average person will dwell on all the obstacles and hindrances which are there to prevent his good coming to pass.

You "combine with what you notice," so if you give obstacles and hindrances your undivided attention, they grow worse and worse.

Give God your undivided attention. Keep saying silently (in the face of obstacles), "Gods ways are ingenious, His methods are sure."

God's power is invincible, (though invisible). "Call unto me and I will answer thee, and show thee great and mighty things which thou knowest not."

In demonstrating our good, we must look away from adverse appearances, "Judge not by appearances."

Get some statement which will give you a feeling of assurance, "The long arm of God reaches out over people and conditions, controlling the situation and protecting my interests!"

I was asked to speak the word for a man who was to have a business interview with a seemingly unscrupulous person. I used the statement, and rightness and justice came out of the situation, at just the exact time I was speaking.

We have all heard the quotation from Proverbs, "Hope deferred maketh the heart grow sick, but when the desire cometh, it is a tree of life." In desiring sincerely (without anxiety), we are catching up with the thing desired and the desire becomes crystallized on the external. "I will give to you the righteous desire of your heart." Selfish desires, desires which harm others, always return to harm the sender. The righteous desire might be called, an echo from the Infinite. It is already a perfect idea in divine mind.

All inventors catch up with the ideas of the articles they invent. I say in my book, *The Game of Life*, the telephone was seeking Bell. Often two people discover the same inventions at the same time. They have tuned in with the same idea.

The most important thing in life, is to bring the divine plan to pass.

Just as the picture of the oak is in the acorn, the divine design of your life is in your superconscious mind, and you must work out the perfect pattern in your affairs. You will then lead a magic life, for in the divine design, all conditions are permanently perfect. People defy the divine design when they are asleep to their good.

Perhaps the woman who liked to lie in bed most of the day and read magazines should be writing for magazines but her habits of laziness dulled all desire to go forward.

The fishes who desired wings, were alert and alive, they did not spend their days on the bed of the ocean, reading *Vogue* and *Harper's Bazaar*.

Awake thou that sleepeth and catch up with your good!

"Call on me and I will answer thee, and show thee great and mighty things, which thou knowest not."

"I now catch up with my good, for before I called I was answered."

Rivers in the Desert

> *Behold, I will do a new thing: now it shall spring*
> *forth; shall ye not know it?*
> *I will even make a way in the wilderness, and*
> *rivers in the desert.*
>
> Isaiah 43:19

In this 43rd chapter of Isaiah, are many wonderful statements, showing the irresistible power of Supreme Intelligence, coming to man's rescue in times of trouble. No matter how impossible the situation seems, Infinite Intelligence knows the way out.

Working with God-Power, man becomes unconditioned and absolute. Let us get a realization of this hidden power that we can call upon at any moment.

Make your contact with Infinite Intelligence, (the God within) and all appearance of evil evaporates, for it comes from man's "vain imaginings."

In my question and answer class I would be asked, "How do you make a conscious contact with this Invincible Power?"

In reply, "By your word." "By your word you are justified."

The Centurion said to Jesus Christ, "Speak the word master and my servant shall be healed."

"Whosoever calleth on the name of the Lord shall be delivered."

Notice the word, "call"; you are calling on the Lord or Law, when you make an affirmation of Truth.

As I always say, take a statement which "clicks," that means, gives you a feeling of security.

People are enslaved by ideas of lack; lack of love, lack of money, lack of companionship, lack of health, and so on. They are enslaved by the ideas of interference and incompletion.

They are asleep in the Adamic Dream: Adam (generic man) ate of "Maya the tree of illusion" and saw two powers, good and evil.

The Christ mission was to wake people up to the Truth of one power, God. "Awake thou that sleepeth."

If you lack any good thing, you are still asleep to your good. How do you awake from the Adamic dream of opposites, after having slept soundly in the [human] race thought for hundreds of years?

Jesus Christ said, "When two of you agree, it shall be done." It is the law of agreement.

It is almost impossible to see clearly, your good, for yourself: that is where the healer, practitioner or friend is necessary. Most successful men say they have succeeded because their wives believed in them.

I will quote from a current newspaper, giving Walter P. Chrysler's tribute to his wife, "Nothing," he once said, "has given me more satisfaction in life, than the way my wife had faith in me from the very first, through all those years." Chrysler wrote of her, "It seemed to me I could not make anyone understand that I was ambitious except Della. I could tell her and she would nod. It seems to me I even dared to tell her that I intended, some day, to be a master mechanic." She always backed his ambitions.

Talk about your affairs as little as possible, and then only to the ones who will give you encouragement and inspiration. The world is full of "wet blankets," people who will tell you "it can't be done, that you are aiming too high."

As people sit in Truth meetings and services, often a word or an idea will open a way in the wilderness.

Of course the Bible is speaking of states of consciousness. You are in a wilderness or desert, when you are out of harmony— when you are angry, resentful, fearful or undecided. Indecision is the cause of much ill health, being unable to make up your mind.

One day when I was in a bus, a woman stopped it and asked the conductor its destination. He told her, but she was undecided. She got half way on, and then got off, then on again: the conductor turned to her and said, "Lady, make up your mind!"

So it is with so many people, "Ladies make up your minds!"

The intuitive person is never undecided, he is given his leads and hunches, and goes boldly ahead, knowing he is on the magic path.

In Truth, we always ask for definite leads just what to do; you will always receive one if you ask for it.

Sometimes it comes as intuition, sometimes from the external.

One of my students, named Ada, was walking down the street, undecided whether to go to a certain place or not. She asked for a lead. Two women were walking in front of her. One turned to the other and said, "Why don't you go Ada?" The woman's name just happened to be Ada, my friend took it as a definite lead, and went on to her destination, and the outcome was very successful.

We really lead magic lives, guided and provided for at every step if we have ears to hear and eyes that see.

Of course we have left the plane of the intellect and are drawing from the superconscious, the God within, which says, "This is the way, walk ye in it."

Whatever you should know, will be revealed to you. Whatever you lack, will be provided! "Thus saith the Lord which maketh a way in the sea and a path in the mighty waters."

"Remember ye not the former things, neither consider the things of old."

People who live in the past have severed their contact with the wonderful now. God knows only the now. Now is the appointed time, today is the day.

Many people lead lives of limitation, hoarding and saving, afraid to use what they have; which brings more lack and more limitation.

I give the example of a woman who lived in a small country town. She could scarcely see to get about, and had very little money. A kind friend took her to an oculist, and presented her with glasses, which enabled her to see perfectly. Sometime later she met her on the street without the glasses. She exclaimed, "Where are your glasses?"

The woman replied, "Well, you don't expect me to hack 'em out by using them every day, do you? I only wear them on Sundays."

You must live in the now and be wide awake to your opportunities.

"Behold, I will do a new thing, now it shall spring forth; shall ye not know it? I will even make a way in the wilderness, and rivers in the desert."

This message is meant for the individual. Think of your problem and know that Infinite Intelligence knows the way of fulfillment. I say the way, for before you called you were answered. The supply always precedes the demand.

God is the Giver and the Gift and now creates His own amazing channels.

When you have asked for the Divine Plan of your life to manifest, you are protected from getting the things that are not in the Divine Plan.

You may think that all your happiness depends upon obtaining one particular thing in life; later on, you praise the Lord that you didn't get it.

Sometimes you are tempted to follow the reasoning mind, and argue with your intuitive leads, suddenly the Hand of Destiny pushes you into your right place, and under grace, you find yourself back on the magic path again.

You are now wide awake to your good, you have the ears that hear (your intuitive leads), and the eyes which see the open road of fulfillment.

"The genius within me is released. I now fulfill my destiny."

INDEX

Further Reading

Books

The Divine Design, Lorie Ladd (self-published, 2022)

The Four Agreements, Don Miguel Ruiz (Amber-Allen Publishing, 1997)

The Game of Life and How to Play It, Florence Scovel Shinn (self-published, 1925)

The Higher Powers of the Mind, Ralph Waldo Trine (Library of Alexandria, 1917)

Infinite Possibilities, Mike Dooley (Simon & Schuster, 2019)

The Power of the Spoken Word, Florence Scovel Shinn (Shinn Press, 1945)

The Science of Getting Rich, Wallace D Wattles (Elisabeth Towne, 1910)

The Secret, Rhonda Byrne (Simon & Schuster, 2006)

The Secret Door to Success, Florence Scovel Shinn (self-published, 1940)

The Shift, Wayne W Dyer (Hay House, 2009)

You Can Heal Your Life, Louise Hay (Hay House, 1984)

Your Forces and How to Use Them, Prentice Mulford (F J Needham, 1911)

Your Word Is Your Wand, Florence Scovel Shinn (self-published, 1928)

Websites

mortentolboll.weebly.com/the-new-thought-movement-and-the-law-of-attraction.html
truthunity.net/books/rebecca-gittrich-whitecotton-seeking-unity/the-new-thought-movement

Wisdom from other law of attraction experts can be found on YouTube, including:

Dr Wayne W Dyer
Esther Hicks and Abraham
Lorie Ladd's *Untangled* show and other videos
Christina Lopes
Caroline Myss
Teal Swan